# A Men's Ministry For the Small Church

Karl W. Kloppmann

Copyright © 2004 by Karl W. Kloppmann

*A Men's Ministry For the Small Church*
by Karl W. Kloppmann

Printed in the United States of America

ISBN 1-594672-40-7

All rights reserved by the author. The contents and views expressed in this book are solely those of the author and are not necessarily those of Xulon Press, Inc. The author guarantees this book is original and does not infringe upon any laws or rights, and that this book is not libelous, plagiarized or in any other way illegal. If any portion of this book is fictitious, the author guarantees it does not represent any real event or person in a way that could be deemed libelous. No part of this book may be reproduced in any form without the permission of the author.

Unless otherwise indicated, Bible quotations are taken from the New International Version Copyright © 1984 by the International Bible Society. Used by permission of Zondervan Publishing House.

www.xulonpress.com

# ACKNOWLEDGEMENT

I wish to thank Jill Bachman for diligently typing and preparing this book for publication.

# DEDICATION

I wish to dedicate this book to my dear wife, Priscilla, who has faithfully served with me in the pastoral ministry all the days of our wonderful marriage.

# TABLE OF CONTENTS

**Chapter One**
    **INTRODUCTION** ................................................................13
        Priority of Men's Ministries
        Overview of the Study

**Chapter Two**
    **WHY DO CHURCHES NEED A MEN'S MINISTRY?** ...19
        Church Suffers from Famine of Male Leadership
        Decline of Male Leadership in the Family in American Society

**Chapter Three**
    **THE NEEDS OF CONTEMPORARY MEN** .....................33
        Walk with God
        Vision
        Good Family Man
        Involvement in Local Church
        Small Groups
        Job Satisfaction
        Mentoring
        Balance

**Chapter Four**
    **THE BIBLICAL BASIS OF MALE LEADERSHIP** .........47
        Gen 2:18
        Gen 2:21,22
        Other Internal Evidence
        Major Objection
        Eph 5:22-24
        I Tim 2:8-14
        Eph 6:4

I Tim 2:2
Christ's Selection of Male Apostles
Old Testament Pattern

**Chapter Five**
   THE DIAGNOSTIC TEST..................................................65
     Random Sample
     Simplicity
     The Problem Stated
     The Basis for the Diagnostic Test
     Conclusions Concerning the Diagnostic Test
     Felt Needs
     Men's Ministry Prior to Diagnostic Test

**Chapter Six**
   THE MEN'S PROGRAM OF FIRST BAPTIST
   CHURCH .............................................................................73
     The Funnel Approach
     The Men's Committee
     Ministries Planned to Meet Needs

**Chapter Seven**
   THE FOLLOW-UP QUESTIONNAIRE ..........................83
     Background
     Follow-Up Questionnaire
     Questionnaire Results
     Basic Conclusions
     Recommendations for Further Study

**Chapter Eight**
   HOW TO START A MEN'S MINISTRY ........................95
     Create Interest
     Develop Momentum
     Build the Program
     Sustain the Momentum

## APPENDIX
- A. CIRCLE OF NEEDS ..................................................... 101
- B. ACCOUNTABILITY QUESTIONS FOR SMALL GROUPS ................................................................ 102
- C. KEYS TO JOB SATISFACTION ................................. 104
- D. UNITED STATES APPRENTICE CERTIFICATE ........ 108
- E. THE DIAGNOSTIC TEST ........................................... 109
- F. DIAGNOSTIC TEST RESULTS ................................... 115
- G. FELT NEEDS TABULATIONS .................................... 118
- H. THE MISSION OF THE MEN'S MINISTRY OF FIRST BAPTIST ..................................................................... 119
- I. PROMISE KEEPERS SURVEY/FATHER/CHILD OUTINGS SURVEY .................................................... 120
- J. FOLLOW-UP QUESTIONNAIRE ................................ 121
- K. RESPONSES TO THE FOLLOW-UP QUESTIONNAIRE ....................................................... 124

## BIBLIOGRAPHY ..................................................................... 125

CHAPTER ONE

# INTRODUCTION

Pastors face the problem of sharpening the focus of their churches. Many churches have a general idea of what they want to do. For example, they desire to edify the saints; so they have some basic ministries, which teach the Word to children and adults. The focus, however, is too general, resembling a shotgun blast. What is needed is a rifle shot approach aimed at specific goals concerning the ministry of the Word. Churches need to focus on specific ways of ministering the Word to specific groups to meet specific needs in the assembly.

To sharpen the focus of ministry in the church will involve the prioritizing of ministries. One of the purposes of this book is to show the logic of a pastor and other church leaders making men's ministry a significant priority.

The church of Christ is effected by contemporary culture in two basic ways. First, the church continually struggles against the pressure of the world to squeeze the church into its mold. An example of this is the divorce statistic. A recent survey of 3,854 adults from 48 continental states established that 25 percent of adults have experienced at least one divorce. The same survey indicated that 27 percent of born again Christians have also experienced at least one divorce (Barna Research Group, 1999, Ventura, California).

In light of the tendency of the church to be conformed to what is going on in the world, there is cause for great alarm when the evidence points to the continual deterioration of marriage and the family in the world. Consider these statistics:

> *The number of intact married couples who rate their marriage as very happy has decreased. In 1973, 67.4% said their marriages were "very happy." That percentage decreased to 61.9% in 1996 (Popenoe and Whitehead, 1999, p. 10).
>
> *It has been estimated that after ten years, only 25% of first marriages are successful, i.e., intact and reportedly happy (Glenn, 1996, p. 18).
>
> *The average median age for marriage is the highest in American history. It presently stands at 27 for men and 25 for women (Popenoe and Whitehead, P. 8).
>
> *The percentage of adults who are presently divorced has quadrupled since 1960 (U. S. Bureau of the Census, *Current Population Reports*, series P20-514; *Marital Status and Living Arrangements:* March, 1998).
>
> *The percentage of children in single-parent families has risen from 9% in 1960 to 28% in 1998 (Ibid., p. 16).
>
> *Thirty-five percent of children now live apart from their biological fathers (Horn, 1998, p. 12).
>
> *In 1980, only 32.3% of teenage girls felt that cohabitation was a good idea. The figure now stands at 54.6%. In 1980, 44.9% of teenage boys felt cohabitation was a good idea, compared with 62% now (*The Monitoring of the Future Surveys,* conducted by the Survey Research Center at the University of Michigan).

*More than 50% of teenagers state that out-of-wedlock childbearing is now a "worthwhile lifestyle" (Ibid.).

*From 1960 to the present, the number of unmarried cohabiting couples has increased 865% (U.S. Department of the Census, "Unmarried-Couple Households, by Presence of Children: 1960-present," January 7, 1999).

*From 1950 to 1980 the annual rate of illegitimate births increased by 450% (Hardenbrook, 1991, p. 379).

*In 1982, the 715,200 children born without fathers represented 19.4% of all births for that year (Ibid.).

*In 1981, over 51% of people arrested for what the FBI considers to be serious crimes were under the age of twenty (MacGillis and ABC News, 1983, p.143).

*American husbands abused six million wives in 1988, four thousand of whom died as a result (Hardenbrook, p. 382).

*On average, American fathers give each of their children a mere three minutes of undivided attention each day (Ibid., p. 379).

As Dobson laments, behind these social trends are millions of hurting people-"husbands, wives, and children for whom everything stable and predictable has shattered" (Dobson, Nov 1999, p. 2).

If the church is to resist the pressure of the world as it seeks to destroy marriage and the family, Christian men must lead the way. If the church's God-ordained leaders are weak, then marriage and the family will fall apart in the church as in the world. But where are the men in the church? Hardenbrook thunders,

> For too long the boys of America have been viewing the church as a sanctuary for women and Sunday School as a place of sissies. For too long the most predictable fact about young males in the church is that the majority of them will leave by the time they are young adults...If we are to remove the curse of father-loss from our land, the church more than any institution on this earth must face the responsibility of turning the hearts of fathers back to their families...Men must again become the primary religious educators of their children...Men must enter the Sunday Schools (Hardenbrook, p. 386).

One way that the church is effected by contemporary culture is by its power to squeeze the church into its mold, but a second way is through the church's need to purge the world out of its converts. Men who get saved are coming out of the world and need the church's help to overcome the anti-marriage and anti-family culture of the world. The church needs to offer ministries especially geared to men to assist them in resisting the pressure of the world to conform and to help them purge the world out of their lives after they get saved.

Some time before her death, comedian Lucille Ball did an interview with talk-show host, Merv Griffin, who asked her a very serious question. "Lucille, you've lived a long time on this earth and you are a wise person. What's happened to our country? What's wrong with our children? Why are our families falling apart? What's missing?" Lucy's startling reply came quickly. "Papa's missing," she said. "Things are falling apart because Papa's gone. If Papa were here, he would fix it" (Ibid., p. 378).

Through effective men's ministries, the church must put Papa back into the family and back into the church. Men must father their families and the church-the family of God.

The spiritual quality of the home and the church depends more on the quality of male leadership than on any other factor. As Morley said, "Jesus intended for the flesh of the church to be hung on the bones of its men" (*A Look In The Mirror*, Newsletter For Men, number 41). The two most important institutions of society, the family and the church, are sharpened by sharpening the men who lead them.

Making men's ministries a priority in the church does not necessitate developing a huge ministry that will dwarf all other ministries. That will not happen because there are many ministries needed in a balanced local church.

There will not be enough manpower, especially in the small church, to build a large, comprehensive program as might be found in a large church.

A good analogy of an effective men's ministry in a small church is the leavening process. A little leaven will leaven the whole lump. An effective men's ministry can be like good leaven. It does not have to dominate everything; it just has to be there in a quality, steadfast way. The men who are continually influenced by an effective men's ministry will positively influence the whole church.

Maxwell and Dorman, stress this principle of leadership:

> If the people you are working to enlarge are part of a group-no matter whether it is a business, church, sports team, or club-then the whole group benefits from their growth. For example, if many people in your organization improve themselves even slightly, the quality of your whole organization increases. If a few people improve themselves a lot, the potential for growth and success increases due to the increased leadership of these people. And if both kinds of growth occur as the result of your enlarging, hang on because your organization is about to take off (Maxwell and Dorman, 1997, p. 126)!

In light of the first purpose of this book, which is to show the logic of making men's ministry a priority, Chapter Two is devoted to establishing the need of a men's ministry in every local church; Chapter Three is devoted to analyzing the needs of contemporary men; and Chapter Four is devoted to presenting the biblical basis for male leadership in the church.

The second purpose of this book is to demonstrate how a church can evaluate and develop a men's ministry from a particular case study. In order to evaluate the existing men's ministry of First Baptist Church, a clear understanding of the needs of the men was needed. This was also needed to further develop the men's program.

On the basis of the contemporary needs of men, which surfaced in surveying current literature on men (Chapter Three), a diagnostic test was devised to reflect these basic needs. The test was given to ascertain where the men of the church stood in relationship to these needs. This information helped the leadership to know how to further develop the men's ministry. Chapter Five is devoted to the Diagnostic Test, and Chapter Six is devoted to the men's program of First Baptist Church. Chapter Seven is devoted to the Follow-Up Questionnaire that was devised to measure whether the program that was developed met significant needs of men, which had surfaced through the Diagnostic Test. Basic conclusions are also drawn concerning the men's program and the tools used to evaluate it. Chapter Eight, the final chapter, shows how to start a men's ministry in the local church.

There is a special need for small churches to develop effective men's ministries. Since the national average for a church is about 120, according to Promise Keepers (March, 1999 Website survey), most of America's churches are small. *Leadership* magazine learned through a survey that 59 percent of small churches had a men's ministry, while 86 percent of large churches did (Winter, 1991, p. 17). The future of small churches across America depends on whether or not they are able to develop effective ministries to men. If they fail, the deterioration of marriage and the family will come into the small church like a flood. Their ministries will not survive without a strong male presence. The writer is convinced that the most crucial ministry for the small church to develop is a men's ministry. At the time of the study, First Baptist Church was slightly bigger than the common definition of a small church (100 or less), but still suffered from the same limitations of the small church. Most small churches will be able to follow the model of men's ministry developed in First Baptist Church of Warsaw, Indiana. This is the reason for this book being titled "A Men's Ministry for the Small Church."

CHAPTER TWO

# WHY DO CHURCHES NEED A MEN'S MINISTRY?

## The Church of Christ in General is Suffering from a Famine of Male Leadership

### Indicators

First, contemporary men are less spiritually inclined than women. This can be seen in the number of books purchased in Christian books stores by women. Bill Hendricks of the Christian Booksellers' Association reported on February 28, 1991, that a recent survey taken of seven different Christian book stores in different parts of the country revealed that three out of four buyers were women (Hughes, 1991, p. 263).

In addition, according to a *Leadership Journal* Survey, the typical church service has 59 percent females in attendance, in contrast to 41 percent male attendees. Further, married women who attend church without their husbands outnumber married men who attend church without their wives four to one (*Leadership*, Winter, 1991, p. 17).

This statistic has serious implications. According to research in the field of men's ministries, when Dad and Mom both attend church regularly, 72 percent of their children remain faithful to the

Lord. If only Mom attends church regularly, 15 percent remain faithful. But if only Dad attends church regularly, 55 percent remain faithful (Rand, 1986, p. 83).

In 1994, 3,795 youth from thirteen denominations participated in the 1994 Churched Youth Survey. This study indisputably revealed the importance of Mom and Dad's church attendance on their children. However, the greater influence of a father again surfaced. Teens and pre-teens who attend church weekly are seven times more likely to have fathers who attend weekly than those youth who attend only monthly or less frequently. Youth who attend church every week, however, are only five times more likely to have mothers who attend weekly (McDowell and Hostetler, 1994, p. 303). A father's spiritual example consistently carries more weight than the mother's example. This of course supports God's choice of the man as the spiritual leader of the home.

The Billy Graham Association did a study, which also supports the stronger spiritual influence of the man. They learned that whenever the father gets saved first, there is a 60 percent chance that the rest of the family will follow his example. If the mother gets saved first, there is a 40 to 50 percent chance that the rest of the family will follow. If a child comes to Christ first, there is a 25 percent chance that the entire family will become Christians (Morley, 1997, pp. 125-126).

Another sign of the special power of a father is the higher rate of delinquency and personality disorders found in children of fatherless families. The ratio of delinquent children living with the mother only compared to those living with the father only is about three to one (Amneus, 1979, pp. 26,64).

A Gallop poll released in 1992 by the National Center for Fathering found that 70 percent of Americans agreed with the statement "the most significant problem facing the American family is the physical absence of the father from the home" (Bauer, 1992, p. 101).

An authority on biblical manhood has summed up the apathy of men today with these words "If I were to put my finger on one devastating sin today, it would not be the so called women's movement, but the lack of spiritual leadership by men at home and in the church. Satan has achieved a tactical victory by disseminating the notion that the summons for male leadership is born of pride and fallenness, when in fact pride is exactly what prevents spiritual leadership. The spiritual lethargy among men today is the crucial issue, not the upsurge of interest in women's ministries" (Piper, 1991, p. 53).

Comparing the demise of the moral values and social institutions of America to the wreckage caused by a great flood, one author lists fifteen deadly currents, which have made up this deluge. At the very top he lists "Men who relinquish their biblical role of leading and providing for their families" (Lewis and Campbell, 1995, p. 24).

✷ Second, there is a high rate of immorality among contemporary men. *Leadership Journal* polled a thousand pastors and learned that 12 percent of them had committed adultery while in the ministry and 23 percent had done something they considered sexually inappropriate (*Leadership,* 1988, p. 12).

A national survey of 4,000 active pastors over a ten year period conducted by counselors at First Evangelical Free Church of Fullerton, California, and completed in 1998, indicated that one in five pastors admits to indulging in "sexually inappropriate" behavior with someone who was not his wife since the time he first became involved with some local ministry (*World Magazine,* Nov 11, 2000).

*Christianity Today* surveyed a thousand of its subscribers who were not pastors and found that 23 percent had committed adultery and 45 percent had done something they considered sexually inappropriate (*Leadership* 1988, p. 12).

In conclusion, one out of five pastors has been involved in immoral conduct and one out of two laymen has been sexually impure. It should be noted that *Christianity Today* readers tend to be leaders in the church. The percentage is probably higher among average laymen in the church.

✷ Third, there has been a decline in marriage, and since men are to be the initiators of the marriage bond (leave father and mother and cleave unto his wife-Gen. 2:21), they must be major contributors to this decline.

In June of 1999, a study was released by the National Marriage Project at Rutgers University titled "The State of Our Union-The Social Health of Marriage in America." The final report began with this overview: "key social indicators suggest a substantial weakening of the institution of marriage. Americans have become less likely to marry. When they do marry, their marriages are less happy. And married couples face a high likelihood of divorce. Over the past four decades, marriage has declined as the first living together experience for couples and as a status of parenthood. Unmarried cohabitation and unwed births have grown enormously, and so has the percentage of children who grow up in fragile families" (Popenoe and Whitehead, 1999, p. 2).

The present trend of cohabitation before marriage has very ominous implications. Studies have shown that cohabitants have an 80 percent greater likelihood of experiencing a marital breakup than those who do not live together before marriage (Barna, 1993, p. 134).

Fourth, there has been a decline in Christian youth. A recent churched youth survey, which was taken under the direction of the Barna Research Group, reported that 55 percent indicated that they had fondled breasts or had intercourse at least once before they were 18 years old. Yet 51 percent could not state that such activity was morally unacceptable. Fifty percent said they were stressed out, 36 percent had cheated on an exam, 20 percent had tried to physically harm someone intentionally, and 55 percent indicated that they were confused about how to tell right from wrong. Fifty-seven percent believe that what is wrong for one person is not necessarily wrong for someone else (McDowell and Hostetler, 1994, pp. 8, 9, 15).

It should be noted that 84 percent of the respondents to the survey said that they attend youth group and Sunday School at least once a week.

This broad, flexible view of ethics is being called the "new tolerance." One author defines "new tolerance" as "the view that every individual's beliefs, values, lifestyle, and perception of truth claims are equal...There is no hierarchy of truth. Your beliefs and my beliefs are equal, and all truth is relative" (Helmbock, summer, 1996, p. 2).

In *USA Today* this statistic was highlighted: "Nearly two in three adults believe ethics vary by situation, or that there is no unchanging ethical standard of right and wrong" (*USA Today,* April 29, 1997).

Traditional tolerance values and accepts the individual without necessarily approving of, supporting, or participating in his or her beliefs or behavior. However, the new tolerance that is being propagated is based on a relative view of truth rather than an absolute standard. It requires a respect and acceptance of other people's beliefs, regardless of what they are. It is estimated that 80 percent of the time when you hear the word "tolerance" used outside the walls of the church today, it almost never refers to a traditional understanding of "tolerance" (McDowell and Hostetler, 1998, p. 18).

It is feared that the majority of young people in evangelical churches today have embraced the new tolerance. For such an unbiblical view of right and wrong to take captive the majority of Christian youth means a clear breakdown of fatherhood. Fathers are to be a powerful influence in the thinking of their children. In the book of Proverbs, the father is depicted as the chief molder of the thoughts of his children (Proverbs 1:8; 2:1; 3:1; 4:1; 5:1; 6:1; 7:1; 10:1; 13:1).

For a generation of youth to develop a distorted view of right and wrong could only happen if that same generation of fathers failed to pass the baton of truth on to their children.

Another harbinger of the spiritual decline of contemporary youth is their flirtation with immorality via the media. The 1994 Churched Youth Survey indicated that 45 percent watched MTV at least once a week. It also indicated that 16 percent watched an X-rated or pornographic movie during the previous three months and 12 percent read a pornographic magazine (McDowell and Hostetler, 1994, p. 258). In harmony with the careless viewing habits of young people is the fact that the average television viewer in a religious home watches four hours of television a day (Barna and McKay, 1984, p. 51). No one will debate that the average television viewer is a young person.

Media expert, Professor Neil Postman of New York University, says that between the ages of six and eighteen, the average child spends some 15,000 to 16,000 hours in front of the TV, whereas he spends only 13,000 hours in school (Nielsen Report, 1986, pp. 6-8).

One of the most absolute but needed statements of our time was made by author-pastor Kent Hughes, when he said, "It is impossible for any Christian who spends the bulk of his evenings, month after month, week upon week, day in and day out watching the major TV networks or contemporary videos to have a Christian mind" (Hughes, 1991, p. 75). It is also equally impossible for any father to allow his children to watch immoral programming, whether it is TV, movies, or magazines, and still be a strong, responsible father at the same time. The careless viewing habit of children is the result of fathers who are not doing their job.

Fifth, men generally fail to take leadership in the church. One way they do this is by absentia. Women comprise 60 percent of the general church population. Many men simply are not present to work or lead in the church. The high rate of divorce has definitely contributed to men who neglect the church. Married women attending without their husbands outnumber men attending without their wives by four to one (*Leadership,* Winter, 1991, p. 18).

In a survey representing churches across the spectrum of size and theological classification, it was noted that over half the churches responding to the survey had women currently serving on the church board or council (Ibid. p.20). Such a trend is the likely result of men unavailable for leadership or unwilling to take the lead.

The writer knows of a Bible teaching church that has a woman for a teacher of an adult Bible study class consisting of an audience of both men and women. Her response has been "I will step down as soon as a man is willing to take the position." So far no man has been willing to take the class.

It is also an accepted fact that the average church is operated by 15 to 20 percent of its membership. On the basis of this principle, an authority in the area of mentoring wrote, "Wherever I go, across America or around the world, the screaming need is for leaders...We need leaders in our churches" (Seven *Promises of a Promise Keeper*, Hendricks, 1994, p. 48). Hendricks was challenging men to assume their leadership role in the church.

Politicians strive to get people to vote in elections. A small percentage of people actually go to the polls. In similar fashion, God is challenging men to get involved in the Lord's work, because only a small percentage of men are involved in participating in and leading the church of Christ.

Echoing this same need, Piper writes, "Where are the men with a moral vision for their families, a zeal for the house of the Lord, a magnificent commitment to the advancement of the kingdom, an articulate dream for the mission of the church and a tenderhearted tenacity to make it real" (Piper, 1991, pp. 53, 54)?

Piper's question indicates that he believes that men are missing from the church in large numbers. It should also be acknowledged that male leadership in the church is not only needed from a practical point of view, but it is also needed from a theological perspective. God's way of building the church is by means of male leadership (1 Tim 2:8-14; 3:1-3). To abandon this pattern is to mock God. Surely His full blessing will not rest upon churches that do not honor, support, and practice male leadership.

## There is a Decline of Male Leadership in the Family in American Society

### Observations

There is a secular men's movement gaining momentum throughout the United States. This movement is parallel to the spiritual awakening that is going on among men today, spurring them to be the husbands, fathers, and spiritual leaders in the church that God desires.

In the secular world there is great interest in masculinity. This can be seen in the success of *Iron John,* a book on what it means to be a man by Robert Bly, 1990. This book was on the *New York Time's* best seller list for 40 weeks. Hedgegard claims that a dozen more on the same theme are on the way. He also refers to 1,500 men's support groups springing up in towns across the nation and popular seminars for men only for $450 a reservation (*McCalls*, Nov, 1991, p. 98).

Evidently due to the feminist movement, many men are

confused about what true masculinity is. Bly's work, *Iron John*, endeavors to rediscover manhood by means of a unique interpretation of a Grimm brothers' fairy tale. Traditional male virtues such as forceful action, initiative, endurance of pain and difficulty, protectiveness, and courage are stressed through Bly's interpretation.

Bly drives home two powerful points. One is that because of the Industrial Revolution, most fathers no longer work alongside their sons. They are absent, working at a job their sons never see. There is too little father in their lives, which means sons have lost their most significant and sometimes only mentor. *Iron John* pictures a boy being mentored into full manhood.

Bly's second point is that modern society has no initiation into manhood, as did primitive cultures. Sons are not taught the secrets of manhood. Our culture does not know how to make men.

Bly makes some good points, but his view of manhood is too narrow. His ideal man has no relationship to God. Plus, the virtues he honors are not sufficient to make a man a good husband and father. In reading the book, the writer cannot recall the word "love" ever mentioned.

In complete contrast to Robert Bly, David Blankenhorn links true masculinity to the term "a good family man" (Blankenhorn, 1995, p. 202). He writes, "Ponder the three words 'Good' (moral values), 'Family' (purposes larger than self), 'Man'" (norm of masculinity). As a phrase of speech, "Good Family Man" was once widely heard in our society, bestowed on men as a compliment and badge of honor. A good family man consistently puts his family first (Ibid., p. 202).

The weakening of fatherhood in our generation has created an unhealthy chasm between fatherhood and masculinity. To be a man to many men does not have anything to do with being a good husband and father. Manhood is identified with violence, materialism, and predatory sexual conduct.

To be a man means: "I will hurt you if you disrespect me. I have sex with lots of women and my girl friends have my babies. I have more money and more things than you" (Ibid., p. 225). "I am a man because I cherish my wife and nurture my children" is not part of the equation of manhood these days.

One of the needs of contemporary men is a true understanding of masculinity; otherwise they will develop an identity crisis. Relating masculinity to being a good family man is on target. Taking Scripture as the guide regarding the true meaning of masculinity, it is clear that no man is a man in God's eyes who fails to be a conscientious father and husband, for God commands men to instruct their children in the Lord's wisdom, exercise appropriate discipline, adequately provide for their family's needs, and love their wives like Christ loved the church (Psa 34:11; Prov 13:24; I Tim 5:8; Eph 5:25). It is wise not to go too far in this direction, however, for single people then could not be masculine. Christ Himself could not be considered a man's man, for he was unmarried.

For the married man, masculinity would demand that he be a good family man, but for the single man, masculinity would include behavior that does not undermine family values, such as sexual purity, financial responsibility, respect for parents, and compassion for the sick, elderly, and unborn.

Between 1992 and 1993, Blankenhorn interviewed 250 parents in eight states. These interviews were conducted in small groups of 9-12. The collective definition of a good family man was:

1. Provider and protector/knows the value of money
2. Shows love of spouse and children through actions
3. Has biblical and moral values
   - spiritual leader
   - good role model
   - good listener
   - takes time for his family
   - balances priorities
   - problem solver, teacher, guidance counselor
4. Flexible/shares workload as a partner

In summation it can be said that a good family man puts his family first.

According to the article *Honor Thy Children,* children are living in a "Fatherless society." Nearly two out of five children in the United States do not live with their fathers. It is calculated that more than half of today's children will spend at least part of their childhood without a father (*U.S. News and World Report*, Feb 27, 1995).

Rutger's sociologist, David Popenoe, is out of step with his colleagues, because he is advocating a revitalization of the traditional family as the cure for poor school performance to soaring crime rates (Robertson, *Insight*, March 14, 1994).

Popenoe and a group of like-minded sociologists are advocating a notion so out of step with their colleagues that many regard them with alarm. Their revolutionary idea: "Intractable domestic problems from poor school performance to soaring crime rates might be mitigated by revitalizing the traditional family" (Ibid., p. 19).

Children in single parent families are six times more likely to be poor and three times more likely to have emotional or behavioral problems as children in two-parent families. Their rates of teenage pregnancy and drug abuse are much higher as well, and they are more likely to drop out of high school. The negative effects continue into adulthood as well. Children from single-parent homes have a more difficult time achieving intimacy in a relationship and in forming a stable marriage. They even have more trouble holding a steady job (Ibid., p. 20).

Surprisingly, the statistics are just as grim for children whose parents remarry after divorce. Only the presence of two biological parents seems to provide the stability most children need during their formative years (Ibid., p. 20).

The father's parenting in conjunction with the mother's can predict if the child will have problems externalizing problems, such as aggression, or internalizing problems, such as depression. The combination of the mother's style of parenting and the father's style is more important than either alone (*USA Today*, March 10, 1994).

When a father leaves the home, the first man in the children's lives has either rejected them or failed them. They will never be the same. "This plague of missing fathers is creating an American male who is confused about his identity and under a great deal of psychological stress, and who ends up lashing out in frustration" (Hardenbrook, 1991, p. 382).

A missing father also does great damage to a girl's self-image.

She receives no positive feedback from her father. Instead of being affirmed and made secure, she seeks male attention in other places-often the wrong places (Ibid., p. 383).

There seems to be more than normal resistance to this new evidence. The clear evidence of the defectiveness of single parenting is clashing with the contemporary belief that "the highest good of human life is unlimited personal freedom (Carlin, *Christianity Today,* May 6, 1994, pp. 35, 36).

The absence of the father in a home also means decreased income, adding to the pressures of a single parent home. The median family income in 1992 of married couple homes with preschool children was approximately $41,000; in single-mother homes with young children, median income was about $9,000 (Blankenhorn, p. 42).

Child support payments do not come close to replacing the lost income of a missing father. Besides, most men, to their shame, fail miserably with child support payments. The chief reason for this failure is a lack of motivation. When a father has a hostile relationship with his former wife and has only a limited, artificial input into the lives of the children, he loses his desire to pay the bill. If that's all there is to his fatherhood, he soon loses interest in paying the bill and in his children.

When a father loses the context of his fatherhood, which is being continually present in a care giving, protecting role, he feels like an ex-father, a "defanged" father, who has been granted permission to visit and pay the bills (Ibid., p. 158). Most men drift away from their children under these circumstances.

The United States Census Bureau finds, based on mothers' responses, that 90 percent of fathers with joint custody pay child support, but only 55 percent with mere visitation rights pay child support. Yet only 14 states officially favor two-parent custody (*Times Union*, Dec 12, 1994).

In support of the declining role of male leaders in the American family are statistics from *Father Facts 2* by Wade F. Horn and the National Fatherhood Initiative (*Worship Magazine,* July-Aug, 1997, p. 10). These statistics are as follows:

*In just three decades, from 1960 to 1990, the percentage of United States children living apart from their biological fathers more than doubled, from 17 percent to 36 percent.

*Today 88 percent of children living with one parent are living with their mother.

*Of these children-whether the result of non-marital birth or divorce-35 percent never see their fathers.

*Twenty-six percent of absent fathers live in a different state than their children.

*More than half of children not living with their fathers have never been in their father's home.

The absent father syndrome was prevalent in another form before the current plague of divorce and broken homes. Balswick claims that because of the Industrial Revolution, men have come to spend less and less time with their children (Balswick, 1992, p. 18). Many fathers fail to express emotion or communicate about things of the heart. They are seen but not really heard, because they have so little to really say. Balswick cites a survey of 7,239 men, where almost none said that they had been or were close to their fathers (Ibid., p. 18).

Today fathers can be physically present but emotionally absent. They strive to be good providers but are unable to emotionally connect with their children. This failure is harmful for both boys and girls, but especially for boys, because their masculinity develops by watching their fathers and experiencing a relationship with them (Ibid., p. 156).

Contemporary fathers are no longer leading and nurturing their families due to divorce, lack of time because of the demands of work, or the cultural expectation of a distant, passive father that has been passed onto them by their fathers. Edwin Cole has accurately described the absence of father as "the curse of our time"

(Cole, 1982, p. 142). This absence includes both physical and emotional absence.

When men come to Christ, this is the web from which they must break free. A strong men's program is needed in every local church to help men grow and develop into the good family men that God desires for them to be.

Patrick Morley, a leader in the current Christian men's movement, believes "if for the last 50 years the church had focused on hiring men's ministers in the same way they have hired youth ministers, would today's father and husband be so ill-equipped for his role as spiritual leader of his home" (Newsletter For Men No. 41)?

If there were more ministries to men, fewer ministries to youth would be needed!

In *Leadership Journal's* survey of churches, it was learned that 86 percent of large churches had men's ministries, but only 59 percent of small churches had a men's ministry. Therefore there is a special need of a men's ministry for the smaller church.

Morley also points out that at the core of Christ's ministry was His ministry to twelve men. Everything that was to come was to come out of the overflow of what was happening in the lives of those men. Christ's "first priority" was building men who would lead their families and His church (Ibid., No. 41). Today churches should have as one of their major priorities the continual development of men.

CHAPTER THREE

# THE NEEDS OF CONTEMPORARY MEN

The aim of this chapter is to specify the genuine needs of contemporary men as they relate to God's Will as revealed in Scripture. In searching current literature on men, eight core needs of men surfaced. Of course there are numerous substrata in each of these basic categories. These eight core needs have been analyzed logically and theologically. To reflect this analysis in a visual way, the eight core needs have been organized into eight concentric circles. (See Appendix A.) Each circle logically and theologically flows into the next circle. The inner circles represent the first target of concern in developing a program for men in the church. They are vital to the others. Although all circles influence all the other circles, the inner circles are the driving force of this model. By thinking logically and theologically, the needs of contemporary men have been prioritized and related to each other. Beginning with the center and progressively working outward, these needs will be covered.

First, at the hub is a man's personal walk with Jesus Christ. As Christ said, "Abide in the vine and you will bring forth much fruit." The richer and more consistent a man's personal walk with Christ is, the greater strength he will have to give to the great challenge of God's plan for his life.

Farrar shares how he asked over 1,000 Christian men across the

United States how often in an average week they interacted with the Lord through Scripture. Forty-five percent reported one time a week or less. The majority of those men were committed, church attending Christians. Farrar's point is that the average Christian man cannot lead his family, because he is malnourished (Farrar, 1990, pp. 115-128). He recommends that men strive to spend time with the Lord at least three times a week for thirty minutes. He uses the analogy of thirty minutes of physical exercise three times a week as necessary for physical endurance. Perhaps the same balance in the spiritual realm would be good for most men. Fifteen minutes in the Scriptures and fifteen minutes in prayer three times a week will keep a man in spiritual shape (Ibid., p. 150). This is a realistic goal for most men. It does not do men any good to set their expectations too high and totally fail. It is much wiser to achieve lesser goals then none at all.

Promise No.1 from the book *Seven Promises of a Promise Keeper* focuses on the need for intimacy with God, by means of personal worship, prayer, and integrity (1994, pp. 17-40). It is no accident that a man's walk with God comes first in the list of seven promises. The most fundamental need of all Christian men is to practice the discipline of Enoch "who walked with God" until God took him (Gen 5:12-24).

"Prayer is like a time exposure to God. Our souls function like photographic plates, and Christ's shining image is the light. The more we expose our lives to the white-hot sun of His righteous life (for say, five, ten, fifteen, thirty minutes, or an hour a day), the more His image will be burned into our character, His love, His compassion, His truth, His integrity, His humanity" (Hughes, 1991, p. 81).

Swindoll claims that the one essential for the success of any organization is leadership. Without it confusion replaces vision, morale erodes, enthusiasm fades-the whole system comes to a halt. This is why he has dedicated himself to Bible study. What leadership is to an organization, the Bible is to him (Swindoll, 1999, Vol. 22, No. 8).

Hybels urges people to practice journaling as an effective means of walking close to God. He practices writing down his thoughts and impressions as he seeks to listen to what God is saying to him (Hybels, 1998, p. 147).

In a Promise Keeper's survey of men taken in June of 1999, 87 percent of 1,133 men responded "strongly agree" to the statement "A man's leadership in his family comes out of a personal relationship with and love for God."

Back to Men of Integrity also surveyed men on the question "What is your biggest barrier to spending time with God?" Fifty-six percent selected "laziness/motivation" and forty-four percent chose "no accountability" (1999).

Cook gives this testimony concerning the priority of walking with God:

> Personal devotions are the stuff of which effective public ministry is made. Faced with a schedule, which often included as many as 8 or 10 meetings a day (I once had 13!), I found that the only way to survive spiritually was to meet with my Lord in the early morning. The busier the day the earlier I needed to arise. Skip that morning meeting with the Lord and the rest of the day would net me very little. But get something fresh from the Lord in the morning and I could share it throughout the day with great effectiveness.
>
> Neglect of personal, private meetings with the Lord led me inevitably to failure. One of the saddest things in the world is to see the decline of a highly gifted ministry-a ministry that is falling to pieces for want of a daily meeting with the Lord. A person in this plight starts to work harder, fails more often, becomes more critical of others, and finally turns to cynicism and bitterness. This kind of decline is both tragic and needless (Cook, 1978, p. 19).

Smith sums up the first priority of a man's life with this observation: "If you think quiet time is passive and tame, you are in for a surprise! Fellowship with Christ is the heart of the whole matter, and He is active" (Smith, 1988, p. 23).

Second, flowing out of the first circle is the need for every Christian man to have a clear vision of what God wants him to be. As a man walks with God by interacting with His Word, God will give him a sense of purpose. God wants men to build solid marriages based on the principles of Scripture. He wants men to nurture and lead their families to know and follow Christ.

Weber contends that every man was made for a cause. He refers to a picture that was reproduced on the cover of *Focus on the Family* magazine, portraying four horsemen riding together. Those men are going somewhere. There was something out there, ahead of them, beyond them. They were men on a mission. They were going for it with everything in them. Focus on the Family ministry had commissioned that painting to commemorate four key men who had been killed in a plane crash. These men were laymen on a mission to save the spiritual values of the whole nation. Every man ought to have an equally clear vision for his life (Weber, 1993, pp. 213, 214).

Sanders writes, "Those who have most powerfully and permanently influenced their generation have been 'seers'-people who have seen more and farther than others-persons of faith, for faith is vision" (Sanders, 1967, p. 55).

Surely Christ is the fount of our best imagination and vision. The finest visions that can possess us come directly from God through Christ. Calvin Miller warns, however, that God does not shout His best vision through hassled Christian living. He gives His visions in the solitudes of life (Miller, 1996, pp. 29, 30).

It would be a good exercise for every Christian man to develop a simple mission statement for his life such as, "to build a dynamic personal walk with Christ, a loving and spiritually nurturing relationship with his wife and children, and a life dedicated to service in the local church." (See *Writing a Life Mission Statement,* available through Man in the Mirror ministries, 180 Wilshire Blvd., Casselberry, FL 32707.)

Third, every man needs to be a good family man. Since Chapter Two focused on the need to be a good family man, further attention will not be given to this need at this juncture, other than to reaffirm that men need to lead their wives lovingly and spend sufficient time nurturing their children (Eph 5:24,25; Eph 6:4).

Since the early 1990s thousands of men attending Promise Keepers Conferences have taken a 228-question profile focusing on felt needs and behavioral practices. When asked to specify their need for help on several dozen topics, assistance to improve fathering skills has ranked 1st or 2nd on the survey every year (*National Survey of Men,* 1993-1998). When God works in the hearts of men, He awakens a passion to be good family men.

Fourth, every Christian man needs to become anchored to a local church. Walking with Christ, maintaining a strong vision, and being a good family man do not occur in isolation from the body of Christ. Every man needs the regular input of the ministry and fellowship of the local church (Heb 10:24,25). He also needs the opportunity to serve in the church. A man who refuses to use his spiritual gift for the common good of the body is not in right relationship to the Head.

Hughes declares that men need the local church, because without commitment her men will not grow. (Hughes, 1991, p. 158.) He also stresses that men need the disciplines of regular attendance, membership, giving, participation, love, and prayer (Ibid., p. 158).

In *Seven Promises of a Promise Keeper,* Promise No.5 reads "A Promise Keeper is committed to supporting the mission of his church, by honoring and praying for his pastor, and by actively giving his time and resources."

Colson writes, "Failure to cleave to a particular church is failure to obey Christ. For it is only through a confessing, local body of believers that we carry out the work of the church in the world" (Colson, 1992, p. 271).

For a man to neglect the local church is like a body part which suffers from poor circulation. Because the blood supply is cut off, the body part fails to receive the nourishment it needs. As Saucy said, "The individual members of the body are channels of nutrition in relation to one another that the body might grow 'with a growth which is from God'" (Saucy, 1972, p. 31).

A man must be vitally connected to the other body parts of the body of Christ, so that spiritual nourishment will flow from the Head through the various body parts to him. Vital spiritual growth is connected to consistent involvement in the life and ministry of the church.

Grudem points out that there are certain activities within the life of the church that God uses to bring blessing to His people. He refers to these "means of grace" as activities that God uses to bless and strengthen us. He does not mean what Roman Catholics mean, by the expression "means of grace"- making people fit to receive justification from God (Grudem, 1994, pp. 950, 951).

Grudem gives the following list of activities that God uses to enable His people:
1. Teaching of the Word
2. Baptism
3. The Lord's Supper
4. Prayer for one another
5. Worship
6. Church discipline
7. Giving
8. Spiritual gifts
9. Fellowship
10. Evangelism
11. Personal ministry to individuals

This is what we miss if we neglect involvement in the local church (Ibid., p. 950). It is impossible for men to neglect the local church and be strong in the Lord for life's demands.

"The church is a big deal to God, and our task is to expand our understanding of and appreciation for the church until it becomes a big deal to us" (Anders, 1997, p. 15). In order for men to spiritually thrive, the local church must become a big deal to them.

There is no doubt that God has raised up the Promise Keepers movement, for it not only is calling men back to their wives and children, but back to the local church. The apex of this renewal is a fresh commitment to honor and support their pastor. How fitting that leaders in the home and church support the leader of the local church. Men who are exposed to Promise Keepers rallies or literature suddenly become aware of the tremendous necessity of supporting their pastors. They promise Christ to build up the most important, but often the most abused man in the church - the pastor.

Bounds wrote, "The men in the pew given to praying for the pastor are like poles which hold up the wires along which the electric current runs. They are not the power; neither are they the specific agents in making the Word of the Lord effective. But they hold up the wires upon which the divine power runs to the hearts of men...they make conditions favorable for the preaching of the Gospel" (Bounds, 1961, pp. 172, 173).

Any program designed to meet the needs of contemporary men must motivate men to take their proper place in the local church and lead their families in the same direction.

Fifth, every Christian man needs a group of men to whom he is accountable.

There has been a small group movement sweeping across the country in the last decade that has not only penetrated the religious community but also the secular. According to *Christianity Today*, "Four out of every ten Americans belong to a small group that meets regularly and provides caring and support for its members. These are not simply informed gatherings of neighbors and friends, but organized groups, Alcoholics Anonymous and other 12-step groups, singles groups, book discussion clubs, sports and hobby groups and political or civic groups" (*Christianity Today*, 1994, p. 21).

First Baptist Church of Warsaw, Indiana hosted a Dad the Family Shepherd Conference. A strong component of this powerful conference was the challenge to become part of a small group of men, who would meet on a regular basis, for the purpose of encouragement and accountability. The men who attended were strongly warned that if they failed to do this, they would most likely fail to make the changes in their lives that they desired to make (Dad the Family Shepherd Conference Manual, 1993, p. 68). In other words, the lasting value of the conference hinged on whether or not the men got into small groups.

Gorsuch states, "growth comes from truth shared through meaningful relationships" (Gorsuch, 1991, p. 14). Richardson writes, "In a small group men experience the challenges of self-disclosure, committing themselves to mutual support and encouragement. Here a man interacts beyond the level of 'what he does' and 'who he is' to a deeper level of 'what he struggles with' and 'how he is going to succeed'" (Richardson, 1994, p. 15). (See Appendix B for a list of the accountability questions used by some men's small groups.)

McGill says, "To say that men have no intimate friends seems on the surface too harsh, and it raises quick objections from most men. But the data indicates that it is not far from the truth. Even the most intimate of friendships (of which there are few) rarely approach the depth of disclosure a woman commonly has with other women...men, who neither bare themselves nor bear one another, are buddies in name only" (McGill, 1985, pp. 157, 158).

This is what is missing from the lives of most Christian men. They lack a network of close friends and support. The small group is highly effective and necessary for men. It provides an ideal structure to practice Proverbs 27:17— "As iron sharpens iron, so one man sharpens another." The New Testament is replete with "one another passages." The small group is the ideal opportunity to fulfill these opportunities to one another.

Smalley and Trent also strongly argue for the need to be part of a small group. Going so far as to say, "If no other message in this book hits home with you, our prayer is that this one will. For from the time Jesus left us to live out the Christian life, He puts us in groups-small centers of support-yet big enough to give us the help we desperately need during times of trouble, and major encouragement for positive growth" (Smalley and Trent, 1992, p. 135).

Small groups are not new. We see them in the early church- "They broke bread in their homes and ate together with glad and sincere hearts, praising God and enjoying the favor of all the people" (Acts 2:46,47).

George Whitefield, the great evangelist and friend of John and Charles Wesley, shared these insights concerning small groups:

> And then tell me, all ye that fear God, if it be not an invaluable privilege to have a company of fellow soldiers continually about us, animating and exhorting each other to stand our ground, to keep our ranks, and manfully to follow the captain of our

salvation though it be through a sea of blood?

What an inestimable privilege must it be to have a set of true, judicious, hearty friends about us, continually watching over us, to inform us where we have fallen, and to warn us, that we fall not again for the future. Surely, it is such a privilege, we shall never know the value thereof till we come to glory (Whitefield, 1832, p. 111).

Besides the benefits of a small group mentioned by Whitefield, Sell adds this one: "Men report that being in a close-knit group of men frees them to communicate more intimately with others. Their communicating skills get better, and they feel more at ease talking to their wives and children" (Sell, 1996, p. 63).

Engstrom supports small groups because of the power of accountability. He writes, "I've noticed that behavior put under close scrutiny tends to change for the better. People who are made accountable to a mentor, to a group of friends, to a therapy group, to a psychiatrist, to a pastoral counselor, or to a prayer group become more serious about changing their behavior" (Engstrom, 1989, p. 33).

Commenting on the need for men to be in a small group, Etter declares, "Simply stated, men are not healthy when they do not experience close relationships with a few other men. Perspective is lost, self-confidence is lost, and I have seen Satan rob many men of their dignity and self-worth" (Etter, Summer, 1997).

Every man would do well to heed these humbling but true words: "A Promise Keeper is committed to pursuing vital relationships with a few other men, understanding that he needs brothers to help him keep his promises" (*The Seven Promises of a Promise Keeper*, 1994, p. 43).

Hendricks warns, "A man who is not in a group with other men is an accident waiting to happen" (Hendricks, June, 1992, p. 3).

We come now to circle No.6-a man's need for job contentment. Many men are frustrated with their jobs. According to Patterson and Kim, "Only 10 percent of American workers say they are satisfied with their jobs" (Patterson and Kim, 1991, p. 155). This detracts from their sense of fulfillment, which erodes their self-esteem. Also, a man suffering from a poor self-image usually does not do well in other areas of life. Sometimes the root of mediocrity as a husband and father is job frustration and emptiness.

Another by-product of job frustration is a lack of confidence to mentor another man. This is one reason why job satisfaction is placed before mentoring in the circle of needs. Unless a man handles his job well, it is unlikely that others will pursue him as a mentor, and it is unlikely that he will have a desire to mentor others.

Every Christian man should experience all joy and peace and hope in his job (Rom 15:13). Sherman writes, "We believe that the workplace is today the most strategic arena for Christian thinking and influence. Moreover, until we become godly workers, we have little hope for becoming godly husbands, wives, parents, or church members. For unless Christlikeness characterizes the 60-80 percent of our lives spent at work, we are simply not living Christlike lives" (Sherman, 1989, p.7). (See Appendix C on how to be content with your job.)

The last twenty years have been years of early retirements and down sizing of corporations. Many men have been left reeling in confusion and shock. In the job world, men need to learn where they fit best and feel good about it.

Circle No.7 is the need for mature men to mentor others. The Lord mentored twelve, and they in turn successfully launched His church. Of the twelve, there were three that He mentored in a special way-Peter, James, and John. These men played special roles in the development of the early church.

Other mentoring relationships in the Bible were: Moses and Joshua, Naomi and Ruth, Elijah and Elisha, Elizabeth and Martha, Barnabas and Saul, Paul and Timothy, and Priscilla and Aquila and Apollos.

Up until the Industrial Revolution, children worked along side their fathers all day long. This created a built-in mentoring relationship between father and son. There are very few natural mentoring relationships today. If older men are to build into the lives of younger men, then these relationships must be intentionally developed.

Bly in *Iron John* builds his theme around a man mentoring a young man into full manhood. He also quotes Robert Moore as having said, "If you're a young man and you're not being admired by an older man, you're being hurt" (Bly, 1990, p. 31). The secular world realizes that the way you make men is to mentor young men.

Hendricks in a lecture titled "Mentoring" shared a number of key insights into mentoring from his own personal experiences. He feels that you must commit yourself to a process of mentoring as well as a person to be mentored. The mentoring process can be very time consuming. Mentoring, however, is essential to having maximum impact in the lives of people.

Hendricks also believes that the person mentored develops according to how the one mentoring him sees him. It is vital to see the potential that people possess. This vision will have a profound influence in their lives for good. Mentors need to believe in people, just as Barnabas believed in Saul, when no one would risk associating with him.

Also, in the lecture, Hendricks listed three essentials of mentoring. First, look for the strengths and affirm them. Second, look where they need to develop and coach them in those areas. Third, look for what needs to be changed. This will involve confrontation, which is always a risk (Dallas Theological Seminary workshop, 1994).

Generally speaking a mentor is:
- a person who has achieved superior rank on an organizational or professional ladder
- an authority in his or her field as the result of disciplined work, study, and experience
- influential in his or her chosen field
- genuinely interested in a protégé's growth and development
- willing to commit time and emotional energy to a relationship with an understudy (goes beyond mere interest and is a commitment that, more often than not, is intense)

On the other hand, there are some things a mentor is not. He is not:
- automatically a pal or a buddy, or one to be included

necessarily in family gatherings or other social functions
- "on call" for grievances and frustrations, imagined or real
- to be gracefully dismissed when the mentoree decides that the relationship is no longer useful- the association has a natural cycle of its own (Engstrom, 1989, pp. 4, 5).

Forman says, "For me, mentoring is a very freeing concept. Sometimes it is necessary to work intensively for a short period with a person in a discipling mode, at other times a few choice words of encouragement and counsel are all that is required." He goes on to say "A few well chosen, affirming words from someone they greatly respect can empower future leaders to scale a mountain for God" (Forman, 1995, p. 5).

Expressing the thoughts of a mentoree, Chuck Colson openly wonders what would have become of him, had he not had a mentor like Doug Coe (Engstrom, 1989, p. 37).

Judging from the shortage of spiritual leaders in the world today, every mature man needs to be mentoring others. Engstrom quotes Ralph Waldo Emerson who wrote, "Our chief want in life is somebody who shall make us do what we can" (Ibid., p. 70). Every mature Christian man should be looking for the men that God is sending into his life to mentor.

The secular world is built on the concept of mentoring. If it weren't for mentoring, we would have no accountants, plumbers, lawyers, doctors, and construction workers.

The United States Department of Labor has a Bureau of Apprenticeship and Training, and the Secretary of Labor has established the basic standards of apprenticeship. People complete apprenticeship programs in various occupations and receive apprenticeship certificates issued by the United States Department of Labor. (See Appendix D.)

According to Webster's Dictionary, to be an apprentice involves "serving another for an agreed period of time in order to learn a trade or business" (Webster's, 1992. p. 50). The Christian world needs to recognize the significance of mentoring, because men need mentors to help them learn the skill of being the spiritual leaders God wants them to be.

All of the seven circles flow into Circle No.8. Every Christian man needs to have balance in his life. Only the fulfillment of Circle No.1 will enable a man to maintain a good balance in his life. In John 17:4, Christ told His Father that he had finished the work the Father had given him to do. The only way that was possible was for Jesus to have perfectly balanced his priorities. Abiding in the vine begins the series of interrelated circles, and in a sense, it ends the circles, keeping everything in perfect balance.

Abiding in the vine will not only strengthen a man to hold to priorities, but it will prompt a man to seek divine wisdom for the difficulties of maintaining a good balance.

Bechtle gives a good example of such wisdom. He states,

> Sometimes we're forced to fix our attention on one area of responsibility. If I'm in a busy period at work, I may not have time for a romantic dinner with my wife. So, until the crunch time is over, the relationship continues to grow with brief, casual conversation, gentle touches, and thoughtful gestures. If I have a major project at work that takes attention away from my family for three weeks, I'll make sure they receive my undivided focus in the days that follow. A three-day weekend camping trip can do wonders for a family's morale, especially if you don't check your voice mail the whole time (Bechtle, 1995, p. 76).

In Europe athletes revere the Pentathlon. It is made up of five diverse events. An athlete must excel in all five events. He cannot do well in one or two and poorly in the other three. He must excel in all five events. He must have a good balance. The same is true for men. They must do well in regard to all of their responsibilities; they must have good balance. Sherman warns men that the greatest temptation they face is to pour all of their emotional energy into work leaving very little left over for non-work responsibilities (Sherman, 1989, p. 30).

An effective men's program in the local church must be geared to meeting these eight basic needs of contemporary men.

CHAPTER FOUR

# THE BIBLICAL BASIS OF MALE LEADERSHIP IN THE HOME AND IN THE CHURCH

> Gen 2:18-The Lord God said, "It is not good for the man to be alone. I will make a helper suitable for him."

The woman is to function as a helper (*ezer*) to the man. The word "helper" defines the role of the woman as an assistant to her husband. She is to help him carry out the commands of God given to him. It is clear from this word that the man is the divinely appointed leader of the home.

As Aaron was given to Moses to help him, so Eve was given to Adam to help him, thus, establishing him as the leader. Although Adam probably helped Eve in many ways, his chief function was the leader, not the helper. This interpretation fits 1 Cor 11:9, "neither was man created for woman, but woman for man."

Out of 21 usages of "helper" in the Old Testament, 16 refer to God as our helper, and God is clearly a superior helper (Stitzinger, 1981, p. 31). Mickelsen argues that because the woman is depicted as a superior helper, the term cannot be a term of subordination (Mickelsen, 1989, p. 183).

On the basis of God being our superior helper, Scanzoni and

Hardesty urge that the woman is superior to the man. This, however, is simply an example of the leader (God) helping His servants. The Gen 2:18 passage is an example of the assistant helping the leader. It should be noted that "helper" is the primary function of the woman in relationship to the man, but God is primarily the leader of man, who secondarily helps him when he has need. Stitzinger observes that the context of Gen 2:18 supports man's need of a human helper, not a divine helper (Ibid.). To compare a divine helper to a human helper is like comparing apples to oranges.

Vos also postulates that the woman is superior to the man on the basis that God told Adam to cleave to his wife (Gen 2:24). According to Vos, usually the lesser cleaves to the greater (Dt 10:20; 11:22; 13:4; Josh 22:5; Ruth 1:14; 2 Sam 20:2; 2 Kgs 18:6). However, there are a number of internal factors, which make it very clear that the man is the head over the woman (Vos, 1968,18,n25).

For example, after God made the woman, He brought her to the man, not man to the woman. Also, in bringing the woman to the man, God gave no explanation to the woman concerning who she was, but left it up to Adam to explain to the woman who she was, thus, making the woman immediately dependent upon the man for leadership. Another internal factor pointing to male leadership was God approaching Adam by himself after the couple had sinned. He held the leader responsible for what had happened (Ortlund, 1991, p. 103).

Male leadership emerges from the other key word of Gen 2:18. God made the woman "suitable" to the man. The Hebrew is *keneged* and carries the meaning of "suitable" or "that which corresponds to." It can also mean "before" or "in front of." The noun form "nagid" means "leader, ruler" (Harris, Archer, Waltke, 1980, p. 550).

Spencer argues that the woman is in front of the man as his leader and superior (Spencer, 1985, p. 24). But such a translation does not fit the context. In Gen 2:20 it says, "But for Adam no suitable helper was found." If *keneged* means "superior," then in naming the animals, Adam was searching for a superior, but the responsibility to name the animals indicated that Adam was superior to them. The idea that Adam was searching for a superior helper among creatures inferior to him does not make good sense.

Also, if *keneged* means "superior to" then it does not fit Psa 119:168, which would read "for all my ways are superior to you," a blasphemous idea. The word *keneged* means "before" or "in front of," depicting the woman as a helper to the man as his equal or counterpart, therefore, the translation "suitable."

Male leadership can be seen in the woman being made suitable for the man and not the man being made suitable for the woman.

> Gen 2:21-22-So the Lord God caused the man to fall into a deep sleep; and while he was sleeping, he took one of the man's ribs and closed up the place with flesh. Then the Lord God made a woman from the rib he had taken out of the man, and he brought her to the man.

This passage of Scripture contains two great facts that support male headship. First, the order of God's creation is significant. Paul used this fact to teach that women should not be in authority over men in the church—"For Adam was formed first, then Eve" (1 Tim 2:13). Ryrie, commenting on this verse states, "Adam was first formed means that he had first an independent existence and could in no way be subordinate to Eve" (Ryrie, 1970, p. 79).

Radmacher makes this observation on the order of creation: "This is an implied reference to the privileges that a first born received in ancient society. These privileges were not given on the basis of inherent superiority but instead on being born first, (Gen 25:27-34; 35:23; 38:27-30; 49:3,4; Dt 21:15-17; 1 Chron 5:12), something controlled by God Himself" (Radmacher, 1997, p. 2044).

Moo indicates that in 1 Tim 2:13, Paul emphasizes the temporal sequence of Adam and Eve's creation—"for Adam, then Eve" (Moo, 1991, p. 190). Gundry and Jewett see this as an indicator that the woman is superior to the man, because creation week followed an ascending order. They argue that woman was God's crowning act of creation (Stitzinger, 1991, p. 29). The response to that line of thought is to regard the context. The context of each passage shows us the meaning of God's order of doing things. When dealing with the basic events of creation week, to be created last meant highest position, but when dealing with the creation of male and female, to be created second meant secondary position.

Second, the woman came from the man. Paul takes this to mean that the man has authority over the woman (1 Cor 11:7-10). The woman is dependent upon the man for her existence, and that dependency must be expressed in life through following male leadership.

"All of humanity comes from one source, Adam. As the source of humanity, Adam is the head and consequently the representative of all" (Foh, 1989, p. 72). This is why Adam is considered the head of the race "in Adam all die" (1 Cor 15:22).

Connected to Paul's logic that the woman is under the authority of the man, because she is from the man, is the distinction that the man is the image and glory of God, but the woman is the glory of man. Grosheide comments, "A man reveals how beautiful a being God could create. A woman on the other hand reveals how beautiful a being God could create from a man" (Grosheide, 1953, p. 256).

Gromacki writes, "She is the greatest creation that God could bring out of the man" (Gromacki, 1977, p. 136). A woman's glory is dependent upon the man, and therefore, the man is the leader.

More specifically, the man reveals the authority or dominion of God, but the woman reveals the authority of man (Hodge, 1974, p. 210). This is why the text says that the woman is the glory of man. She manifests his rule and authority, whereas, the man displays the rule and authority of God.

Paul in saying that the man is the image and glory of God, but the woman is the glory of man, was not teaching that the woman does not reveal God's image or glory. She does (Gen 1:26,27), but in the restricted sense of authority and dominion, she does not reveal that aspect of God's glory the way the man does. Therefore, Paul required a woman to reflect the authority of the man over her by wearing a veil in the worship services (1 Cor. 11:7-10).

**Other Internal Evidence from the Creation Account**

The human race was named after man not woman. The text of Gen 5:1 reads "When God created man, he made him in the likeness of God. He created them male and female and blessed them. And when they were created, he called them 'man' (Adam) not 'woman'." God named the human race after Adam in particular, strongly suggesting his leadership over the race. Grudem relates this act "to the custom of a woman taking the last name of the man when she marries: It signifies his headship in the family" (Grudem, 1994, p. 463).

Ortlund, seeing the significance of God's act in naming the race "Adam," says, "After all, if any of us modern people were to create a world, placing at its apex our highest creature in the dual modality of man and woman, would we use the name of only one sex as a generic term for both? I expect not" (Ortlund, 1991, p. 98). When God named the race "man," he was whispering male headship (Ibid.).

Adam named his wife. Just as Adam's act of naming the animals was considered an act of sovereignty over them, so his naming his wife was an act of sovereignty over her. The parallel to naming the animals is striking. God brought the animals to the man to see what he would name them. Then, God brought the woman to the man, and he named her.

The man initiates the marriage bond. In Gen 2:24, we read, "For this reason a man will leave his father and mother and be united to his wife, and they will become one flesh." Note it is not the woman's responsibility to initiate the severing of parental bonds and the establishing of marital bonds, but it is the man's responsibility. The man is active, whereas, the woman responds to his action. Again we see the man in the role of the leader and the woman in the role of the follower.

God's definition of marriage also reveals that men and women are the same in basic nature (one is not superior to the other), but different in function. The man cleaves unto his wife and they become "one flesh." For Adam to join himself to a lesser creature would have been degrading to himself (Ibid., p. 103). Adam could only become "one" with someone who was identical in nature with himself. He himself made that clear when he said, "This is now bone of my bones and flesh of my flesh."

The woman is every inch the man's equal in terms of the quality and nature of her being, but she is functionally not equal to the man.

This can be seen in God giving the responsibility of establishing a new household to the man, not the woman, because this is the responsibility of the head (Ibid.).

The same kind of reality exists in the Trinity of God. God the Father, God the Son, and God the Holy Spirit are coequal in glory and nature (ontological Trinity), but unequal in roles, the Father leads, the Son submits to the Father's leadership, and the Holy Spirit submits to both (economic Trinity).

## Major Objection to Male Headship

> Gen 3:16-To the woman He said, "I will greatly increase your pain in childbearing; with pain you will give birth to children. Your desire will be for your husband and he will rule over you."

Some scholars interpret this passage to teach that the headship of the man over the woman is a post-fall phenomenon. The headship role of the man is the result of sin, and is therefore done away in the redemption of Christ.

Bilezikian, commenting on Gen 3:16 says, "As a result of Satan's work, man must now master over woman, just as the mother-ground was now master over men. For these reasons, it is proper to regard both male dominance and death as being antithetical to God's original intent in creation. Both are the results of sin, itself instigated by Satan. Their origin is Satanic" (Bilezikian, 1985, p. 22).

Jewett says, "We have rejected the traditional view-which affirms the headship of man...The historic rivalry between the sexes which has characterized fallen humanity, a rivalry in which the man has subjugated the woman, treating her as an inferior, and in which the woman has taken her subtle revenge, is done away in Christ" (Jewett, 1975, p. 171).

Proponents of this view (Bilezikian, Jewett, Mickelsen, Spencer) cite Gal 3:28, "There is neither Jew nor Greek, slave nor free, male nor female, for you are all one in Christ Jesus." No one is the head with the right of final decision. In areas of married life where an agreement cannot be reached, some approach must be voluntarily adopted, but there is no final authority in the marriage (Ibid., p. 132). The same kind of application is made to the church. No positions of authority can be denied women. Mickelsen argues,

> Are restricted roles for men and women in church, family, and society God-ordained, or are they the result of sin and/or cultural influences? Some writers in this book believe they are God-ordained; I believe they are the result of sin and/or cultural influences...Christian men and women are not to be entangled in a yoke of bondage. Men and women are to preach. Women and men are to make disciples. They are to minister with the gifts of the Spirit... Restrictions placed upon the full exercise of those gifts have handicapped the church through the ages and kept the gospel from going forth in its full power (Mickelsen, 1989, pp. 173, 205).

If Gen 3:16 were the only verse indicating the submission of the woman to male headship, egalitarian logic would be much more appealing. There is solid evidence, however, for male leadership prior to the fall, which has previously been presented. Then what does Gen 3:16 mean? The verse speaks of the woman's desire and the rule of her husband over her in the context of judgment for disobeying God. The best explanation is that this verse is simply a statement of fact. God was reminding the woman that the subordinate principle still remained in effect. Despite the spiritual fall and corruption of her husband, the woman would still positively desire her husband, and her husband would still be her head.

The word "desire" is the Hebrew word *shukah* and can refer to both a positive and negative desire (Gen 4:7). It seems best to interpret "desire" as a positive desire in light of Song 7:10, which expresses the positive desire of Solomon for the Shulammite woman. Even though women are fallen creatures, it seems extreme to characterize their desire for their husbands as destructive in nature.

Even though her husband will be depraved, she still will be

positively drawn to him and must still submit to his headship, even though it may be harsh and selfish. Because of the sinfulness of the woman and the man, the woman often struggles with being in submission to her husband, and he often struggles with leading her in a gentle, loving way.

It also needs to be noted that the egalitarian interpretation of Gal 3:28 is inaccurate. The context of the passage is dealing with sonship not roles, or positions of service (cf. v. 26). When it comes to our spiritual standing before God, there are no differences. We are all equal and one in Christ before God. This passage does not teach that earthly distinctions are non-existent. Kent, commenting on Gal 3:28 states, "The New Testament provides considerable regulations for the church on earth regarding the varying responsibilities of husbands and wives, their relative positions in the functioning of the local assemblies, and the duties of slaves and masters toward each other. But so far as the essential character of the body of Christ is concerned 'ye are all one in Christ Jesus'" (Kent, 1976, p. 107).

> Eph 5:22-24-Wives, submit to your husbands as to the Lord. For the husband is the head of the wife as Christ is the head of the church, His body, of which He is the savior. Now as the church submits to Christ, so also wives should submit to their husbands in every thing.

Male headship is taught in two ways in this passage. First, the husband is referred to as the head of the wife. The word "head" is the Greek *kephale*, which means "superior rank" (Arndt and Gingrich, 1979, p. 431). The general context of this passage supports the concept of having authority over someone. In Eph 1:22, Christ is the head of the church, which means "God placed all things under his feet" (v. 22a). In Col 2:10, Christ is the head over every power and authority.

There are some who contest that the word *kephale* means "source" rather than "head" or "leader," e.g., Mickelsen, Payne, Bilezikian, and Kroeger. This proposed meaning is very questionable. Grudem did a study of 2,336 instances of *kephale* from a wide range of ancient Greek literature. He could not find one convincing example where *kephale* meant "source" (Grudem, 1991, p. 425). Grudem also states that "all the major lexicons that specialize in the New Testament period give the meaning 'to have authority over,' whereas none give the meaning of 'source'" (Ibid.).

Egalitarians make much of Liddell and Scott's lexicon of classical and Koine Greek from 1000 B.C. to about 600 A.D., which did not give "authority over" as a legitimate meaning (Liddell and Scott, 1968, p. 946).

They also focus on two rare uses of *kephale* found in Herodotus 4:91 and Orphic Fragment 21a, both of which are more than 400 years before the time of the New Testament (Grudem, p. 425). Both examples are debatable as to whether or not they mean "source."

Liefeld concurs with Grudem in his claim that Liddell and Scott specialized in classical Greek, not New Testament Greek (Liefeld, 1989, p. 219). He also points out that for "detail on the New Testament period one consults Arndt and Gingrich before Liddell and Scott" (Ibid.).

Grudem dismisses the Liddell and Scott omission as an oversight that needs correction (Grudem, p. 426).

Foh feels that if the idea of source is included in the meaning of *kephale,* it still does not eliminate the clear, common meaning of "authority over" (Foh, 1989, p. 86).

The traditional meaning of *kephale* as "head" in the sense of "having authority over" makes the best sense in the biblical texts under discussion. For example, according to Eph 1:22, before Christ became the head of the church, He had to be exalted to the right hand of God "far above all rule and authority, power and dominion, and every title that can be given." If "head" means "source" or "origin" why was it necessary that He be exalted above all rulers and powers in order to be their source or origin? They were already in existence before Christ's exaltation. If "head" means "to have authority over" then the point is that the one who has authority over the church also has authority over all other powers. As Jesus said, "All authority in heaven and on earth has been given to Me" (Matt 28:18). Because Christ is head over all things, His church cannot be stopped!

A parallel passage also emphasizes "authority over," "Therefore God exalted Him to the highest place and gave Him the name that is above every name, that at the name of Jesus every knee should bow in heaven and on earth and under the earth" (Phil 2:9,10).

Since the man's headship over his wife is parallel to Christ's headship over His church, male headship must mean "to have authority over."

The second way male headship is taught in this passage is through the submission required of the wife. The word "submit" is *hupotasso,* which means "to subordinate yourself to another person" (Arndt and Gingrich, 1957, p. 848). Mandatory submission indicates that she is under the authority of her husband.

The concept of submission is sometimes understood to mean only a general kind of thoughtfulness toward others. Because Eph 5:21 says "Submit to one another out of reverence for Christ," verse 22 is softened to mean that the wife is to submit to her husband in the same way that the husband is to submit to his wife. In other words, a gracious attitude replaces the authority of the husband. Bilezikian writes, "We conclude that mutual subjection...renders hierarchical distinctions irrelevant within the Christian communities of church and family" (Bilezikian, 1985, p. 156).

But this approach does not fit the passage, which goes beyond mutual submission and requires the wife to submit to her husband in everything. There is more going on in this passage than a kind, flexible attitude toward others. The wife is morally bound to submit to her husband's headship.

This approach also does not fit other examples of the word *hupotasso:*

1. Jesus submits to parents (Lk 2:51).
2. Demons submit to disciples (Lk 10:20).
3. Citizens submit to governmental authorities (Rom 13:1,5).
4. Church submits to Christ (Eph 5:24).
5. Servants submit to masters (Titus 2:9).

In Scripture none of these relationships is ever reversed or made mutual. The word is always used in a one directional sense when it refers to submission to a specific authority. It is true that the authority of masters over slaves has been done away with, being a temporal, cultural practice. The other authorities are God-ordained and have permanent, biblical roots.

> 1 Tim 2:8-14-I want men everywhere to lift up holy hands in prayer, without anger or disputing. I also want women to dress modestly, with decency and propriety, not with braided hair or gold or pearls or expensive clothes, but with good deeds appropriate for women who profess to worship God. A woman should learn in quietness and full submission. I do not permit a woman to teach or to have authority over a man; she must be silent. For Adam was formed first, then Eve. And Adam was not the one deceived; it was the woman who was deceived and became a sinner.

The context indicates that Paul had in mind the public worship services of the church. Men are to lead in prayer "in every place." This goes beyond Ephesus and indicates that Paul is laying down basic principles for all churches.

It is also clear by his instructions on how women should dress, that he is not talking about home life, but public life. In this context the public life is going to the worship services of the church.

In the setting of the church service, it needs to be understood that a woman is not depicted as the one leading the ministry of the Word. Rather, she occupies a submissive, learning position (verse 11). When Paul said, "I do not permit a woman to teach," he was referring to public meetings of the church, when a teacher would teach the Word to a mixed audience. Such teaching was an authoritative presentation of the Word, which would call upon people to obey the Word (2 Tim 4:2). House explains,

> In New Testament times "teaching" was not considered merely the dispassionate imparting of

information to which we have become accustomed in our day. Instead, a teacher imparted a way of thinking and living, which he challenged the learner to follow, similar to the function of the elder as explained in 1 and 2 Timothy and Titus. The teacher would also exercise his authority to hold believers accountable (House, 1989, p. 14).

Teaching of this nature is done today by the pastor and by adult Bible teachers who teach both men and women. As Schlatter says, "A woman who taught would give orders to a man. And that Paul does not permit, for she should not rule over men" (Schlatter, 1914, p. 120).

In 1 Tim 2:12, women are restricted specifically from authoritative Bible teaching over men, and generally from exercising authority over men in the church. Teaching is a narrow form of exercising authority over men. Exercising authority over men is a general term, which includes serving as an elder, or holding a position on the governing board of a church.

The Greek *authentein* means "to have authority over" (Knight, 1984, p. 154). Although it is tempting to conclude that "teaching" and "exercising authority" are the same event, it is best to view them as closely related but distinct in meaning. Moo states, "while *oude* joins two closely related items, it does not usually join together words that restate the same thing" (Moo, 1989, p. 187). Paul goes from the specific to the general. Teaching along with all other forms of exercising authority over men in the church is forbidden.

Moo also observes that in the Pastoral Epistles, teaching always has this restricted sense of authoritative doctrinal instruction (1 Tim 4:11; Titus 2:15) (Ibid., p. 185).

Egalitarians respond to the view of male headship in 1 Tim 2:8-14, by arguing that women in Ephesus were caught up in heretical teaching at the time of Paul's writing. Thus, as a temporary measure, Paul forbade women to teach the Word in the public services of the church (Brauch, Bruce, Davids, Kaiser, 1996, p. 666).

There are many problems with this view. First, if false teaching by women is what Paul was dealing with, it seems unfair to apply the instruction to all the women in Ephesus and only the women in Ephesus. Surely, not all the women in the church were heretical. According to Acts 18:24-28, Priscilla and Aquila were from Ephesus (Barron, 1990, p. 456).

Second, Paul's blanket statement, "I do not permit a woman to teach," sounds universal. If Paul would have wanted to contextualize his restriction why did he not simply say, "For the present time, I permit not a woman to teach" or "In Ephesus, I permit not a woman to teach" (Ibid., p. 455)?

Third, Paul's restrictions on female leadership in the church are not based upon anything temporal, such as, a wave of false teaching, but rather on timeless principles grounded in history, such as the order of creation and the fall of Eve (Swindoll, 1989, p. 34).

The creation order has already been analyzed, but what is Paul's point in linking the fall of the woman to the restriction on women? Stress is placed on the woman being deceived and consequently falling into sin. There are three basic views on why this was cause for her not being allowed to teach.

1. A woman should not hold a position of authority over men in the church, because she is more vulnerable by nature to deception (Wemp, 1983, p. 2499). In other words, she was not designed by God to function in that role.

2. A woman should not hold a position of authority over men in the church, because when she did, it did not work. God did not bless the couple when His plan of leadership was violated (Litfin, 1983, p. 736).

3. A woman should not hold a position of authority over men, because the woman fell first. The restriction was a consequence of her fall. Just as Adam faced the consequence of the ground being cursed for his sake, Eve's consequence for falling

included having the door of leadership over men closed to her (Swindoll, Ibid., p. 34).

View No. 3 is clearly wrong. Since the order of creation established the man as the leader, the door of leadership was already closed to the woman. It would have been meaningless to close a door already closed to the woman. The point of the passage is not that the woman cannot be the leader because she sinned, but that she should not be the leader because she has not been equipped by God for that task. Thus, vindicating God's choice of Adam as the leader.

Views Nos. 1 and 2 are very similar. They both suggest that a woman should not be a leader over men, because she has not been equipped to do that well. The woman is more vulnerable to poor judgment than the man, not because of inferiority, but because she was designed by God to play a different role. What is her role in the local church? Learning in quietness (1 Tim 2:11), which is the exact opposite of authoritative teaching, is her role, along with submission to male leadership (vv. 11,12), which is the exact opposite of exercising authority. A woman can serve in multitudes of ways in the local church (Titus 2:3-5), as long as she honors the role given to her by God (1 Tim 2:11,12).

Also, in 1 Cor 14:33-35, Paul places the woman in a submissive role in the public meeting of the church. Women are not permitted to interrupt a worship service to ask a question, but are to ask their questions to their husbands at home. This indicates that male leadership in the church service was not to be hindered by women, but rather to flow smoothly without interruption. A woman's questions were to be answered in the home by her spiritual leader, her husband. Paul is not restricting all verbal expression of women in the church service (1 Cor 11:5), only the disruption of publicly asking questions in the worship service (Mitchell, 1983, p. 2325).

Further corroboration of male headship in I Tim 2:11-12, is the following passage, I Tim 3:1-5. In this passage, Paul requires the overseer who exercises authority in the church, and also teaches, to be a male. In I Tim 3:1-5, Paul was applying his teaching of 1 Tim 2:11-12.

> Eph 6:4-Fathers, do not exasperate your children; instead bring them up in the training and instruction of the Lord.

In this verse, the father is depicted as the head of the family. In Eph 5:22-6:9, three examples of submitting to authority are given. In each example, those who are to submit to authority are addressed first. In the first example, wives are told to submit to their husbands (Eph 5:22). In the second example, children are instructed to obey their parents, specified as "your father and mother" (Eph 6:1). In the third example, slaves are exhorted to obey their masters (Eph 6:5). Then, those who are in authority over wives, children, and slaves are addressed. In Eph 5:25, husbands are exhorted to love their wives. In Eph 6:9, masters are told to treat their slaves with respect. In Eph 6:4, fathers are taught to bring their children up in the Lord. Even though both mother and father have joint authority over their children, Paul singles out the father, because he is the ultimate head of the home. As Boice states: "It is significant that Paul addresses fathers specifically for the simple reason that the responsibility of managing a home and raising children is primarily theirs" (Boice, 1997, p. 21).

It is possible to understand the word "fathers" as meaning "parents" for in Heb 11:23 the same Greek word is translated "parents," but as Kent points out "It is not likely it is so used here, in as much as 'father' was used in its usual sense just 2 verses earlier" (Kent, 1971, p. 108).

Paul addressed the father exclusively, because he is the apex of authority in the family, having authority over his wife and children.

Even though fathers have the ultimate responsibility for teaching in the home, the mother is also responsible to teach her children the way of the Lord. She is entitled to equal honor (Eph 6:2) from her children, and her teaching is equally binding on her children (Prov 1:8; 6:20; 10:1; 15:20; 17:25; 19:26; 20:20; 23:22, 25). In these verses father and mother are both mentioned, but in every reference the father is mentioned first, emphasizing his role as primary leader of the home.

> 2 Tim 2:2-And the things you have heard me say in the presence of many witnesses, entrust to reliable men, who will also be qualified to teach others.

In this text Paul used the word *anthropos* to refer to men. It is a broad word often meaning "mankind" or "human being," but it can also be used to refer to men in contrast to women, as Matt 10:35; 19:5; 1 Cor 7:1 illustrate (Arndt and Gingrich, p. 68, 2b). In 2 Tim 2:2, when Paul speaks of equipping men to teach, he must be using *anthropos* in the sense of males, for only men (males) are permitted to be authoritative teachers in the church (1 Tim 2:11, 12).

Towner feels that *anthropos* refers to believers both male and female (Towner, 1984, p. 170). Mounce argues, "It seems unlikely that Paul is thinking of men and women alike-more likely male elders (1 Tim 3:2), since they were the teachers in the congregation" (Mounce, 2000, p. 506). Quinn and Wacker favor this possibility as well (Quinn and Wacker, 2000, p. 635).

Timothy was to teach the Word to the whole body of believers. But he was also to select faithful and capable men and impart to them the apostolic doctrines. The baton of the faith was to be passed onto the leaders of the church (men), who would in turn pass it onto others. The word "others" is *eterous* which is masculine in gender. Commenting on *eterous* in 2 Tim 2:2, the noted Greek scholar, Alford wrote, "not merely believers but trustworthy men" (Alford, 1958, p. 377). In summation, Timothy was to make a special effort to indoctrinate men, who in turn would indoctrinate other men. This is true apostolic succession-the body of apostolic faith passed on from generation to generation by faithful, competent men-the leaders of the church of Christ.

### Christ's Selection of the Apostles

Christ chose the apostles to represent Him on the earth after His ascension. They represented Him and spoke with His authority. In I Cor 14:37, Paul declared, "If anybody thinks he is a prophet or spiritually gifted, let him acknowledge that what I am writing to you is the Lord's command." John elevated the teaching of the apostles to the level of God. Christ invested in them His authority. According to Ryrie, it is very significant that no woman was chosen to be among the twelve apostles (Ryrie, 1970, p. 32).

Borland contends that Christ was not averse to breaking social customs. When moral issues were at stake, Christ refused to bend to cultural expectations. He ate with sinners, spoke to the Samaritan woman, healed on the Sabbath, and ate with unwashed hands. Had he wanted to, Jesus could have chosen women to be a part of the apostolate. He could have chosen six men and their wives to be His apostles, but no such arrangement was initiated (Borland, 1991, pp. 120, 121).

Christ set the pattern of male leadership in His church by laying male leadership for its foundation.

## The Old Testament Pattern

The Old Testament pattern consistently reflects male leadership. Culver points out that every official feature of the Old Testament theocratic system was in the charge of men. For example, the priesthood was wholly composed of male descendants of Aaron, the brother of Moses. Also, genealogical lines are ordinarily traced only through the male line, and women's vows were not to be binding unless confirmed by the silence of her husband when he should hear of it or, in the case of a minor daughter, "in her father's house in her youth." The vow could be "disallowed" only if the husband or father expressed himself so "in the day that he heareth." In the case of a widow or divorced woman "every vow...should stand" (Culver, 1989, p. 78).

Newer concludes that God chose male leadership in both the Old and New Testament periods, because leaders represent Him, and He is male and His Son is male. God in Scripture is exclusively depicted in male terms, such as "Father," "Lord," and "King." It is only natural that He be represented by men and not by women (Newer, 1991, pp. 153,173,192,193). This is true, but it is never mentioned in Scripture as a reason for God selecting men to be leaders in the family and church. Perhaps the emphasis should not be on why God ordained male leadership, but on the obvious fact that He has.

In conclusion, the Scripture consistently presents the doctrine of male leadership in the family and in the church. Although women are often very gifted and very godly, they are not permitted to hold positions in the church, which require them to teach men the word of God or exercise ruling authority over men. A biblically based ministry will be rooted in male leadership and nourished by significant ministries designed to develop men who are competent to lead their families and their churches.

# CHAPTER FIVE

# THE DIAGNOSTIC TEST

Seventy questionnaires were sent to the men of First Baptist Church. (See Appendix E.) There was no way of predicting who would fill out the questionnaire. Twenty-six were returned (37%). The test was anonymous. Therefore, it was the equivalent of a random questionnaire. An expert in research design, Paul Leedy, made this statement:

> Random samples from populations display in general the same characteristics as the parent population from which they were selected. There are, of course, slight deviations in every sample; samples are not facsimiles of the parent population. But the deviations, if the sample has been selected with adequate randomicity so that it is truly a representative sample, are presumably not of such magnitude as to be significantly different from the population from which the sample was drawn (Leedy, 1985, p. 136).

In light of the high degree of randomicity of the survey, there was a strong confidence that the responses truly represented the seventy men from which the sample was drawn. However, as Leedy points out, "the larger the sample, the more the sample mean approximates the population mean" (Ibid., p. 178). A 37% return is a safe guide, but not a perfect guide.

The percentage of 37 percent is calculated on the basis of 26 responses. Dr. Richard Dilling, Professor of Mathematics at Grace College, Winona Lake, Indiana, shared with the writer in a phone conversation, November 11, 1999, that 30 percent is a typical response to such surveys and that 37 percent was a good response. Dilling has experience doing surveys in the community.

This is in accord with the survey of *Leadership* magazine conducted in the winter of 1991. A thousand subscribers were sent a survey on sexual demographics and 30 percent responded. On that basis the people of *Leadership* put confidence in their survey.

The study of statistics is not an exact science. It is rather a reasonable way to infer what the whole of something is like on the basis of the study of a representative part. For example, astronauts brought back rocks from the moon (samples), and from these samples scientists have been able to infer what the total surface of the moon is like.

## Random Sample

The diagnostic test was sent out to survey the spiritual state of the men of the church. All of the men who received a survey were on the attendance roll of the church. Most attended with some degree of regularity, while some were fringe and others were in nursing homes. The survey was sent to everyone as a courtesy, even though it was anticipated that certain ones would not respond. The survey was titled "Diagnostic Test for Men in the 90s."

All of the responses were truly random responses. It was the equivalent of gathering 70 men together and asking for 26 volunteers to do the survey. The men who returned the survey were in reality volunteering to do the survey. In order to encourage a response, a self-addressed envelope was included with the survey. Also, to encourage a response and truthful answers, the test was designed to be taken anonymously. However, there had to be a way to track the surveys so that follow up surveys could be sent out for the purpose of measuring any progress. In order to accomplish this each respondent was to have his own PIN number (personal identification number). The PIN number consisted of the last four digits of their social security number added to the year of their birth, e.g., 3022+1946=4968. The survey still remained anonymous, but the PIN number could be used to track following surveys.

It was crucial that the test be anonymous. If personal identity had been requested, the responses would have been restricted to a smaller number. Also, many personal questions would have not received honest answers.

## Simplicity

The diagnostic test (survey) was thorough, but as simple and brief as it could be. As Leedy says, "The questionnaire should demand as little effort and time on the part of the respondent as possible" (Ibid., p. 136). It consisted of 40 questions. Most questions required simple responses like yes or no, true or false, or circle the best word. A few scale questions like, "rate your experience from 1-10" were incorporated. Most of the scale questions were placed at the end rather than at the beginning so not to discourage men from taking the rest of the test. For example, the writer recently received a lengthy questionnaire in the mail, which consisted of all scale questions. The writer did not respond because of the time and effort required to complete the questionnaire.

The men were told in advance that it would take about 15-20 minutes to complete the questionnaire. Most men, however, probably completed the test in 10 minutes or less.

## The Problem Stated

Churches do not really know the needs of their men. When it comes to ministering to the needs of their men, the average church needs to sharpen the focus of their men's ministry. The leadership of the church has never studied the needs of contemporary men. Therefore, they do not know what questions to ask their men in order to discover where they stand in relationship to those needs. It is not even enough to know the basic needs of modern men. What is needed is knowledge of the unique needs of the men of the church in relationship to the basic needs of contemporary men. In some groups a great need might be to establish close friendships with a few men, but in other groups that might not be a great need. Instead, another group might have an unusually strong need to live consistently at work. Another church may have a large number of men struggling in their marriages, or a large number of men who are strong in working in the church but weak in walking with God. The problem is: Most churches do not know what the exact needs of their men are, and therefore, they do not know what kind of a program will truly meet their needs.

The question we endeavored to answer was: "What tool will help the leadership learn what the unique needs of the men of First Baptist Church are and help them to plan a better ministry for the men by further developing the ministry in light of those needs?"

The expected answer was: "A men's ministry based substantially on a diagnostic test, which will enable the leadership to further develop the men's program of First Baptist Church with increased effectiveness." It was expected that a ministry based upon the unique needs of the men of First Baptist Church would, upon evaluation, show evidence that those unique needs were being met in a noticeable way. The tools needed were: a diagnostic test to see what kind of ministry was needed; a follow-up questionnaire to see if that kind of ministry had been effective, along with other minor surveys to test the specific effectiveness of certain ministries.

### The Basis for the Diagnostic Test

Prior to developing the diagnostic test, a survey of current literature revealed the recognized needs of contemporary men. These needs were presented in Chapter Three of this book. They were analyzed from a logical and theological perspective. Questions for the diagnostic test were based on these established needs of men.

Apart from an accurate understanding of the needs of men, it is impossible to know what questions to ask. If a person goes to a lab and asks to be tested in order to see if he is healthy, someone will administer a blood test, which will check the blood for certain elements and levels, which have been established as indicators of health.

The questions on the survey were designed to probe these basic needs. Out of 40 questions, 39 specifically dealt with the circle of eight basic needs. Using the eight needs as a reference point, the specific questions, which probed those needs, have been noted. Some questions were applicable to more than one need (See Appendix A for the eight circles of need.)

1. Questions  1,2,3,4,5,6,7,8,10,----------Walk With Christ
   11,12,28,29,38,39

2. Questions  9,35 ---------------------------Personal Vision

3. Questions  5,13,14,15,16,17,18, ------Good Family Man
   38,39

4. Questions  24,25,26,27,28,39 -------Church Involvement

5. Questions  9,20,21,22,23,37------------------Small Group

6. Questions  29,30,31,32-------------------Job Contentment

7. Questions  29,30,31,32------------------Mentoring Others

8. Question  36-----------------------------------------Balance

Realizing that a man's walk with Christ is his greatest need, the survey had the most questions dealing with this need-15. The need to be a good family man was reflected in nine questions. The need for local church involvement could be seen in seven questions. The need to be in a small group had six questions. Job contentment was reflected in four questions. Personal vision and mentoring others each had two questions. There was one question on balance. Needs that had few questions were not unimportant, but rather, they could be assessed in fewer questions. It was also important to keep the survey as brief as possible.

The results of the Diagnostic Test can be found in Appendix F.

**Conclusions Concerning Diagnostic Test**

In order to be classified as a significant need, there had to be at least a 20 percent negative response to a question. Questions that received less than a 20 percent negative response were not interpreted as reflecting a significant need. The lowest negative response to a question was 23 percent and the highest was 95 percent.

On the 1-10 scale questions, there had to be a score of six or less, before it was classified as a significant need. However, there were other factors taken into consideration regarding certain scale questions. For question 13—"On a scale of 1-10, rate your marriage" there were five out of 26 who scored six or under and six who did not answer the question. Those factors seemed to offset the 7.6 overall score, and therefore, marriage was classified as a significant need in the men of First Baptist Church. Also, for question 17—"On a scale of 1-10, when it comes to spending effective time with your kids, score yourself," there were nine that did not answer. This factor, plus an overall borderline score of 6.4, pointed to a significant need. There were some older men who took the test, and they may have passed on the question, because their children were grown and living a distance away.

The diagnostic test revealed that the most significant needs of the men of First Baptist Church were:

WALK WITH GOD
- 29% have quiet time twice a week or less
- 31% describe their spiritual growth as non-existent, meager, or sporadic
- 56% describe their thought lives as either often contaminated to somewhere in between often contaminated and seldom contaminated
- 66% said they very seldom or never witness
- 29% said they experienced no spiritual victories in the last year
- 23% said they were not excited about their Christian lives
- 47% indicated that they give 9% or less of their income to God

## VISION OF WHAT GOD WANTS FOR THEIR LIVES
- 36% have none

## GOOD FAMILY MAN
- 56% struggle with their thought lives
- average marriage score was 7.6-but six did not answer and five scored six or under
- 35% seldom say romantic things to their wives
- average score of spending effective time with children was 6.4, but nine did not answer

## CHURCH INVOLVEMENT
- 58% attend two services a week or less
- 36% have no job in the church
- 47% give 9% or less

## SMALL GROUP INVOLVEMENT
- 85% said they were not in a small group
- 85% said they have no close male friends
- 38% said they do not regularly receive encouragement from other men
- 34% said they do not regularly encourage other men

## MENTORING
- 95% said they were not being mentored by another man
- 88% said they were not presently mentoring another man

## JOB SATISFACTION
- 30% said they were not satisfied with their jobs
- 32% said they were frustrated with their jobs
- 47% are not excited about their future in secular work

## Felt Needs

Question 40 was very revealing- "What do you feel are your two greatest needs at this time?" The felt needs expressed by the men were not always consistent with the diagnostic test. For example, the men of First Baptist seldom put down as one of their two greatest needs vision, small groups, male friendships, mentoring and being mentored, and job satisfaction. Yet, the diagnostic test revealed that the men of First Baptist had significant needs in those areas. Part of the problem with men is that they do not recognize what their true needs are. This makes ministry to men especially difficult.

Most of the felt needs expressed in response to question 40 fell into these three categories:
1. personal walk with God
2. being a good family man
3. local church involvement

(See Appendix G for full tabulation of felt needs.)

## Men's Ministry Prior to Diagnostic Test

Question 37 asked the men to score the men's ministry existing at the time of the diagnostic test. A scale of 1-10 was used- 1 being the lowest- 10 being the highest. The average score was 5.1, indicating that the men's ministry was having impact. One response to question 37 added these words to his score of 8: "Before 1992 I would have put a 4 or 5." It was 1992 that the writer came to the church and began building the men's ministry. The diagnostic test was given in 1997.

The diagnostic test revealed that the men of First Baptist Church had significant needs in seven of the eight needs of contemporary men. It was decided to plan ministries that would help men in these specific areas, with special emphasis on the three felt needs which the men put down the most: walking personally with God, being a good family man, and working in the local church.

CHAPTER SIX

# THE MEN'S PROGRAM OF FIRST BAPTIST CHURCH

The results of the diagnostic test helped to sharpen the focus of the men's ministry. Before the diagnostic test ministries were launched in some general areas, but they were not as specific or purposeful as they should have been. Things were done but there was no clear understanding of why they were being done. Not only was direction needed but also a strategy was needed, because a strategy of ministry helps to maximize the effectiveness of the ministries that are planned.

**The Funnel Approach**

The concept of a funnel was chosen to be the basic strategy of the men's program at First Baptist Church.

The top of the funnel is wide. It represents ministries that are relatively easy for a man to become part of, for they require little commitment to Bible study and relationships. For example, at the top of the funnel, the leadership placed large, special events like Promise Keepers, a city wide Dad the Family Shepherd Conference, a Family Life Conference, special musical concerts, special events at the church, and an annual golf outing, etc. Next down the funnel, large groups were placed, like men's breakfasts, men's softball, father/child outings, men's fish fry, and men's work projects.

Training opportunities were placed next on the funnel, like a Lifestyle Evangelism Seminar, a Dad the Family Shepherd Video Conference, Leadership in the Local Church Seminars, Teacher Training offerings, and Sunday School Conferences.

On the last level of the funnel, E-(encouragement) Teams were placed. These were small groups of men that met regularly together for mutual edification and encouragement. They required commitment to Bible study and the members of the group.

The further a man came down on the funnel, the more exposure he had to the Word and relationships with other men. The top of the funnel events were easy entry points into the men's ministry and the church, plus, they built momentum for events at the bottom of the funnel. They funneled men into ministries designed to produce growth. It was the top of the funnel events that fed the bottom of the funnel events.

### The Men's Committee

Another aspect of the strategy needed to develop the men's ministry was the formation of a men's committee. It was determined that the men's ministry was a significant priority and warranted a special committee to oversee it. Having a men's committee would ensure that an ongoing program would be developed with the specific needs of the men in mind.

The men's committee was organized consisting of six men, including the pastor. The term of service was for two years. By creating a men's committee, a structure for purposeful planning was permanently established. Also, when men come together to discuss men's ministries, it adds to the enthusiasm and momentum needed to maintain and continually develop such a ministry.

Another fruit of the men's committee was new opportunities for service. This helped meet one of the specific needs that surfaced through the diagnostic test-the need to be involved in the work of the local church. Thirty-five percent of the men said that they did not have a job to do in the church. Two of the men who came on the committee had no other involvement in the ministry of the church.

The committee developed a mission for the men's ministry (See Appendix H for diagram representing the mission of the men's

ministry of First Baptist Church.) The purpose of the men's ministry was to provide the *SON* for every man. *S* stands for *salvation*; *O* stands for *other men; N* stands for *nurture*. When men had the *SON,* they would be able to fulfill the specific purposes of the men's ministry of First Baptist Church, which were:
1. Walking with God
2. Leading their families
3. Building their church
4. Making a living
5. Having a testimony

The eight circles of need were also integrated with the diagram of the mission of the men's ministry. For example, circles five and six, small groups and mentoring, correspond to the various aspects of nurture listed under *Son.*

## Ministries Planned to Meet Specific Needs
### Newsletter

In order to create an atmosphere of sustained interest in men's ministries, it was decided to connect all of the men with a newsletter titled *Lifeline.* This is a quarterly newsletter published by Men's Life of Grand Rapids, Michigan. Arrangements were made for this newsletter to be sent to all of the men in the church without charge. It consisted of challenging articles that prodded and encouraged men concerning their responsibilities and needs as men. This newsletter can now be accessed at <www.menslife.org>. The Diagnostic Test revealed that 36 percent of the men said they had no vision of what God wanted for their lives. The newsletter was made a part of the men's ministry to help meet the significant need of vision in the men of the church.

In a telephone conversation with Marjo Jordan of Men's Life Ministries, producer of *Lifeline* Newsletter, it was learned that in the year 2000, the readership grew every quarter. In a survey done by *Lifeline* in 1997, the men indicated that they appreciated the practical tips for men and the format which makes fast reading possible. *Lifeline* is a proven tool for men's ministry (telephone conversation of December 12, 2000).

## Promise Keepers

Because the Promise Keepers rallies were noted for their power to instill fresh vision in the lives of men and also for their ability to help men in their walk with God, their marriages, their children, and their need to draw close to a few other men, it was decided to make these rallies an annual event. In 1998, a simple survey was taken to determine the impact of Promise Keepers rallies. (See Appendix I.) Out of a possible high of 10, the men scored an average of 9.3, rating the power of the worship, the large gathering of men, the messages, and the fellowship with the men that they traveled with to the rally.

## Golf Tournament

Although this event was open to men, women, teens, and even children, it was primarily planned to give men an opportunity to make friends with other men and invite unsaved friends. The Diagnostic Test indicated that 31 percent of the men had no close friends, 46 percent were not able to draw close to other men in the church, and 66 percent said they seldom or never witnessed for Christ. The golf tournament created an opportunity for these needs to be fulfilled.

## Men's Breakfasts

These were held at local restaurants or catered at the church for the purpose of helping men get to know each other, and equipping them to be better husbands and fathers. For example, at one breakfast the program consisted of certain men sharing what had worked well for them in their marriage or with their children. The program at another breakfast consisted of selected men each sharing the contents of a chapter from James Dobson's book, *What Wives Wish Their Husbands Knew About Women* (Tyndale House, 1975).

## Father/Child Outings

These were strictly for men and their children. The outings were to Fort Wayne Wizard baseball games. This event was designed to give men an opportunity to have a fun time with their kids. It also was an opportunity for men to get to know other men and invite other men and their children. In 1999, a survey was given to the men who had recently attended a father/child outing. On a scale of one to five, the men were asked to score the outing's effectiveness in giving them an opportunity to spend quality time with their children and in giving them an opportunity to get to know other men. Out of a possible high of five, the average score was 3.8. (See Appendix I.)

## Work Projects

The men's committee became aware that one of the widows of the church needed a great deal of painting to be done on her house. The men's committee sponsored a special "paint a widow's house" project. This was an opportunity to be involved in God's work and bond with other men. Samsel said, "Working on a project with the single goal of glorifying God helps build friendships that are set on the firmest foundation" (Samsel, 1996, p. 69).

## Men's Softball

This was an activity already in existence, but after the Diagnostic Test, it became more than just a recreational opportunity. The softball team was an entry point into the church and the men's ministry. It also was an opportunity for men to build friendships with other men. Unlike some of the other events, which provided an occasional opportunity to get to know other men, this opportunity lasted week after week for the summer.

## Friendship Evangelism Seminar

The men's committee promoted and organized a Lifestyle Evangelism Seminar, conducted by the International Bible Society. Since one of the significant needs of the men was a need to witness to the lost, this seminar was planned to motivate and equip the men of the church to witness in the context of natural friendships with people. It was open to women as well.

## Pastor's Prayer Support Team

An effort was made to cultivate committed prayer warriors to support the pastor in prayer. Seven people were found who were willing to commit themselves to praying for the pastor one day a week. Each one was responsible to intercede for the pastor on one specific day of the week. The pastor in turn regularly sent these people his top seven requests. With each updated list of seven requests, each prayer warrior also received a summary of how the previous seven requests had been answered. Six men and one woman committed themselves to this ministry. This ministry was designed to empower the pastor's ministry but also to give people an opportunity to be involved in doing God's work. Such involvement helped people to see God work in response to prayer, and helped them to draw near to their pastor.

Forty-six percent of the men on the Diagnostic Test said that they failed to draw near to other men in the church in the past year. To be on the pastor's prayer support team was a way to draw near to their pastor. Although the pastor's prayer team was designed for men, the woman who was accepted on the team was a true prayer warrior of the church. The idea for this ministry came from an incident recorded in Ex 17:11,12, when Aaron and Hur held up Moses' hands to heaven, giving God's people victory over the enemy. Battle weary pastors need to be held up by prayer warriors in order to have spiritual victory over satanic resistance. The Pastor of First Baptist Church affirmed the power of the intercession of his prayer support team, as many long-term prayer requests were answered. He also testified of the special closeness he felt with each of his prayer warriors.

Etter wrote, "Of all the effective men's ministries of which I have been a part or have observed, there have been many common denominators, but one which I have only recently realized is that they all have a strong pastor's support team. I have come to believe that having a pastor's support team is an essential building block for church based men's ministry" (Etter, *Lifeline*, June, 1996).

## **Widower's Support Group**

The leadership felt that of all the men needing to get to know each other, the men who had lost their wives in death had a special need. Four to five widowers and the pastor got together for lunch several times. There was a brief Bible study and each man was asked to share what was particularly difficult for him in being a widower. In conversations with each of these men, it was learned that these support luncheons were greatly appreciated by all participants. The fellowship and the sharing of a common problem was an encouragement to them.

## Small Groups

Small groups was a ministry that could meet multiple needs within the fellowship. It was designed for both men and women as a form of caring for each other and mentoring each other. Most men participated in small groups with their wives, so the involvement nurtured them as a couple and gave them opportunity to nurture other couples. Small group benefits such as intimacy with others, mutual care, and couple enrichment also coincided with some of the significant needs of men that surfaced on the Diagnostic Test. Forty-six percent said they did not draw close to any other men in the last year; 38 percent said they did not regularly receive encouragement from other men; 34 percent said they did not regularly give encouragement to other men; 95 percent said they were not being mentored by another man, and 82 percent said they were not mentoring another man. These needs of the men of First Baptist Church were not totally met by couples bonded together in a small group, but to a degree these needs were met.

Small groups also met the need of marital enrichment. A small group may not be studying marriage or raising children, but a couple's relationship is often nurtured in a small group setting. Couples caring for each other strengthen the joy and satisfaction of being a couple.

At the time of the Diagnostic Test, 85 percent of the men of the church said they were not in a small group. Although the men's committee did not initiate the ministry of small groups, it clearly fulfilled one of the significant needs of the men of the church. The men's committee was solidly behind the small groups ministry, because it recognized small groups as a significant need of the men and the church.

## Encouragement Teams

Encouragement teams were small groups of men that met

together on a regular basis for mutual care, fellowship, encouragement, and accountability. First Baptist Church had two E-Teams of 5-6 men each. These were combined into one larger group of 10-12 men for the purpose of showing some video series. The men seemed to enjoy the larger group so that continued. In order to help the men to have a vision of what God wanted them to be and to help them be good family men, good church men, and good on the job men, the men's committee purchased the video series "A Man of His Word" featuring Dr. Adrian Rogers (Samson Ministries, Dallas, Texas). The series covered these topics:
1. Called to Believe- A Man in Christ
2. Called to Love- A Man and His Wife
3. Called to Nurture- A Man and His Children
4. Called to Serve- A Man and His Church
5. Called to Labor- A Man and His Career
6. Called to Manage- A Man and His Money
7. Called to Lead- A Man and the Market Place
8. Called to Stand- A Man and His Mission

A workbook also was provided for each man to fill out as he viewed the video. This aided in discussion times and provided permanent notes for future reference.

Another resource was used for a period of time titled *Promise Builders* by Homer Ralston (1995, Promise Keepers). The study focused on the major needs of walking with God, being good family men, working in the church, and building relationships with other men.

## Sermon Series

One of the felt needs of the men of First Baptist Church was the need to get more involved in the ministry of the church. Also, 37 percent of the men said they did not have at least one job in the church. These statistics indicated that the pulpit could be used to meet the needs of the men and the needs of the church as a whole, for lack of involvement also characterized the church. The pastor in response to this need did a significant series of messages from Ephesians 4, titled "Life in the Body." The series was designed to challenge the people to use their spiritual gifts. Although the series was well received, only one man is known to have decided to get involved in ministry in response to the series. In response to the challenge of faithful stewardship of spiritual gifts, he committed himself to the youth ministry and became one of the primary leaders.

From the time of the Diagnostic Test, February 1997, to the Follow-Up Questionnaire of 1999, these thirteen ministries made up the men's ministry of First Baptist Church. The purpose of the Follow-Up Questionnaire was to determine whether the men's program of 1997-1999 had met the significant needs of the men.

## CHAPTER SEVEN

# THE FOLLOW-UP QUESTIONNAIRE

**Background**

It was decided not to give the same diagnostic test of February 1997 in February of 1999 for these reasons:
   1. Two years is a long time. It is unlikely that the men would have recalled what they had put down on the first test. For example, on a question like "score your marriage from 1-10 (ten being the highest)" most men would not remember how they scored it on the first test. A man might think to himself on the second test "My marriage is better than before, I think I will give it a seven." Yet, on the first test he gave it an eight. Not having the first score as a reference point would be a real handicap.
   2. The first test although helpful did not give enough choices. For example, Question No.3 was "Do you have a sense that you are growing in your Christian life?" The answer to that question is helpful in an initial diagnostic test, but it would not be a good question to use in measuring

progress in a follow-up test, because the answer will not reflect any degree of growth. Question No.29 "I live a consistent Christian life at work" (T or F) is another example of a question helpful on a diagnostic test, but not specific enough to be used on a test for progress. Although the Diagnostic Test of 97 had a number of specific questions, it was decided that there were too many general questions for it to be used in the Follow-Up Questionnaire.

3. In a random, anonymous survey there is no way to control who will respond. Would the same 26 respond on the second test as did on the first test? If a different 26 responded the second time, then the second test would not measure progress. As it turned out, only seven who took the first test also responded to the second test. It was felt that a test was needed that would simply measure whether the ministry from 1997-1999 had met significant needs in the men of First Baptist Church.

4. On the Diagnostic Test there were many revealing questions, in keeping with the primary purpose to see where the men of First Baptist were in relationship to the basic needs of contemporary men. Therefore, there was only one question designed to measure the impact of the existing men's ministry. It was decided to develop a follow-up questionnaire that would measure progress in terms of the men's ministry. If the same Diagnostic Test of 1997 would have been used again in 1999, whatever progress would have been detected could not have been clearly credited to the men's ministry of First Baptist Church, because there was only one question out of forty linking where the men stood spiritually with the men's ministry of First Baptist Church.

## Follow-Up Questionnaire

The Follow-Up Questionnaire was sent to a smaller group than the group who received the Diagnostic Test. (See Appendix J.) The Diagnostic Test was sent to 70 men, whereas, the Follow-Up Questionnaire was sent to 56 men. Although church attendance stayed approximately the same between the two tests, men come and go. Some men moved away, others died, and some left for one reason or another. Plus, there were a few whom we passed over because of a total lack of interest. The goal of the Follow-Up Questionnaire was to measure the impact of the men's ministry. Those who had shown no previous interest could not help do that.

Out of 56, 19 were returned making a 34 percent response. Once again the survey was anonymous, and again the men were asked for a PIN number, which was calculated the same way as on the Diagnostic Test of 1997 (date of birth plus the last four digits of their Social Security Number). The questionnaire was also sent with a self-addressed stamped envelope.

Anticipating the response, "Oh, no, not another survey!", the questionnaire was shortened to 12 basic questions.

The questionnaire was prefaced with three boxes to check: I have not been involved in any of the men's ministries; I have been occasionally involved in the men's ministries; I have often been involved in men's ministries.

To accurately measure the men's ministry, it was important to know whether the respondent was meagerly exposed to the men's ministry or abundantly exposed. A higher impact would be expected from someone abundantly exposed than from someone with a meager exposure. It would be comparable to asking someone who rarely attends a particular church to evaluate it compared to someone who continually attends. There is no way to put the two evaluations on equal footing. More weight must be given to the evaluation of someone who is abundantly exposed. Those who marked that they had not been involved in any men's ministry were asked only to answer questions nine and ten. The answers to these questions helped us to understand some of the needs of men who were not part of the men's ministry. All of the questions, except for questions nine and ten, were specifically related to the men's ministry of First Baptist Church.

### Follow-Up Questionnaire Results

Of the 19 that came back, five were from men who were not involved in the men's ministry at all. Therefore, they only answered two questions-nine and ten.

Of those who sent back questionnaires, seven were matches from the first Diagnostic Test. Two of the seven were not involved in men's ministries at all. Three of the seven were often involved in men's ministry, and two were occasionally involved. All seven showed at least one area of improvement compared to the test of 1997. For example, pin #9729 indicated on the diagnostic test that he had no close male friends and that he had not grown close to any other men in the church in the last year. On the Follow-Up Questionnaire, however, he indicated that he had been able to meet and get to know other men through the men's ministry of First Baptist Church.

Question No.4 on the Follow-Up Questionnaire stated,

> "Through involvement in the men's ministry, I made this definite change in my life _____."
> Seven shared specific changes that they had made in their lives through the Men's Ministry. For example, one man wrote, "I have become more open and less reclusive."

Of the seven who shared specific changes, six checked that they had often been involved in the Men's Ministry and one checked that he had occasionally been involved.

### More Results Of Follow-Up Questionnaire

1. Getting to know other men through men's ministry, yes-93%
2. Greater awareness of my needs through men's ministry, yes-79%
3. Men's ministry impact on desire to grow, 6.9

out of a possible score of 10 (cf. 8.1 of those often involved in men's ministry)
4. Invite unchurched friends to men's activities, yes-36%
5. Became a better husband through men's ministry, yes-79%
6. Became a better father through men's ministry, yes-79%
7. Healthy contentment with job, yes-79% (cf. No.30-Diagnostic Test of 97-70%)
8. Becoming bolder to witness at work, yes-77%
9. Coping better with job pressures through men's ministries, yes-71%
10. Encouraged through men's ministries, 6.5 out of a possible score of 10 (cf. No.37 on Diagnostic Test of 97-basically the same question with an average score of 5.1, indicating growth in the impact of the men's ministry of First Baptist Church)

The results of the Follow-Up Questionnaire indicated that the Men's Ministry of First Baptist Church of Warsaw, Indiana, from Feb 1997 to Feb 1999, had been effective in meeting many significant needs of the men of the church.

Note Appendix K for the chart of responses to the Follow-Up Questionnaire. At the side of each question, the specific circle of need dealt with by the question is listed.

## Basic Conclusions

First, the men's ministry helped men even though they were only involved in a limited way. The Follow-Up Questionnaire indicated that there were some who checked they were only occasionally involved in men's ministries but still had significant needs met. The temptation in men's ministries is to focus totally on ministries that require maximum involvement, but this is a mistake, for some men can be significantly influenced by occasional events. These types of events are worthwhile in themselves, but they also spark interest in other, more demanding ministries. Every men's ministry needs occasional events to maintain a sustained interest in the men's ministry.

Following special occasional events, like Promise Keepers Events, Father/Child Outings, there was always a surge of renewed interest in men's ministry at First Baptist Church.

Second, men were helped the most by being frequently involved in men's ministries. The Follow-Up Questionnaire clearly revealed a correlation between the impact of the men's ministry and degree of exposure to it. (Greater exposure equals greater impact.) The chart of the responses to the Follow-Up Questionnaire shows a clear pattern of higher responses from those who were often involved in men's ministry. (See Appendix K.)

Most of the men who checked that they were often involved in men's ministry had reference to involvement in E-Teams, because the other men's ministries were occasional, whereas E-Teams were regular. E-Teams were also the most often mentioned in question five. The men were asked to name a particular event sponsored by the men's ministry that was especially helpful to them. E-teams or particular studies offered in E-Teams were mentioned more than any other event.

Because of the correlation between frequent involvement and spiritual impact, it is clear that men need to be involved in small groups of men. Included in the concept of a small group of men would be a close male friendship, or a mentoring relationship. A small group consisting of men and women is acceptable, but it does not take the place of a small group made up of just men. In a men only group, men are free to talk about their needs, problems, and weaknesses in a way that is not true of a mixed group. Every man ideally needs a small group of men to kindle, keep alive, and fulfill his vision to be the man God wants him to be.

Consultant Pat MacMillan surveyed over 2,500 Promise Keepers who had kept their promises. He asked them, "Who helped you keep them?" The two overwhelming answers given were, "my wife" and "my church-based small group" (Morley, 1999, No. 92).

Rand also testifies that the men's small group ministry accomplished more than any other aspect of the men's program of his church (Rand, 1986, pp. 217, 218).

Small groups of men seem to be a new phenomenon, although the Lord had a small group of men, and Paul had a small group of associates with whom he ministered, and the local churches had groups of men in leadership called "elders." According to a Promise Keepers survey of 1,048, taken in 1999, men's small groups at that time had usually been in existence on an average of five years (PK Website: Men in Groups Survey, March 1999).

Third, a significant number of men who got involved in E-Teams at First Baptist Church, subsequently got involved in other ministries of the church. Ten men got their start in the church's ministry through E-Teams. Of the ten, one became a deacon, another moved and helped start a men's ministry in another church, two men with pastoral background became pastors of local churches, and the rest took on leadership roles in children's church, youth ministry, Awana Clubs, and small groups (mixed). E-Teams fed the total ministry of First Baptist Church.

Fourth, the reason why there was a steadfast men's ministry at First Baptist Church is because there was one particular man with a passion for this ministry. The Pastor of First Baptist Church founded and developed the men's ministry. Behind every effective men's ministry in a local church, or parachurch ministry, is a man with a passion to see men become the leaders in their homes and churches that God wants them to be. Of all the possible and worthy ministries a pastor could focus on, a vital, steadfast men's ministry is one of the most strategic.

Fifth, over a period of time a small men's ministry can have a big impact. Christ had a men's ministry for twelve men, and those twelve men became the foundation of the church. The New Jerusalem is built upon twelve foundations, named after the twelve apostles. This is Christ's eternal tribute to the men He used to build His church (Rev 21:14). A small group of men in any ministry can have a great impact. A men's ministry does not have to be large to be powerful, because men are leaders and they will influence others and others will influence others.

Sixth, rather than mailing out the surveys, it would have been wiser to give them out at a large gathering of men. The men would have immediately filled them out and handed them in. This would have secured a much greater response. Such a gathering might be a morning worship service. The service could be dismissed fifteen minutes early and the men could be asked to stay and do the survey. If the church has a comparable women's program, a survey could be given to the women at the same time. The survey could still be mailed to those who were absent that particular Sunday.

Seventh, in mailing out surveys and asking for a response by a certain date, it would have been wise to send out a reminder postcard shortly before the response date. Many men did not respond to the surveys, because they set them down and forgot about them.

Eighth, the Follow-Up Questionnaire should have been longer. In light of small groups beginning in the church, there should have been a question or two regarding its impact. There should have been a question or two on increased involvement in the ministry of the local church, since this was one of the felt needs reflected in the 1997 Diagnostic Test. A question or two on personal devotions and church attendance would also have been appropriate.

Ninth, the Diagnostic Test of 1997 should have had more specific questions. For example, one True/False question read, "I have some weaknesses that I need to get victory over in my life." A better question would have been "Name two weaknesses that you need to get victory over in your life." Or, this multiple choice question could have been used: "Circle the area or areas where you need to get victory in your life: marriage, children, church involvement, walk with God, job, relationships with others, witnessing, and maintaining priorities."

Another example of a need for specificity would be the statement: "When it comes to spending effective time with your children, score yourself from 1-10 (10 being ideal)." The word "effective" is too general. A better statement would have been "The time I spend with my children is drawing us closer together," score yourself (1-10).

Also, "I am taking time to teach my children the Word of God" would have been a more specific True or False question.

Tenth, more scale questions, like "score yourself from 1-10," should have been used. The True/False statement, "My passion in life is to be the man God wants me to be in my family, in my church, in my job, and in my community" would have been better as a scale question. A man might give himself a five, another a nine or ten. If the choice were simply True/False, the difference between a five and a ten would be missed. The one who would score five would likely mark true, as would the one who would score ten. Yet, there would be a significant difference between the two men. One would have a mild passion to be the man God wants him to be, but the other would have a very strong passion.

## **Recommendations for Further Study**

First, the Follow-Up Questionnaire of 1999 revealed a clear correlation between the degree of involvement in the men's program and the degree of impact the program had on a man's life. For the men of First Baptist Church the greater exposure was in connection with the E-Teams. It would be significant to know if the high impact of E-Teams is universal across the country. Do men who regularly attend a small group of men experience a greater rate of spiritual growth and development than men who are not involved in small groups? A survey dealing with this question would have to be sent out to many churches with men's ministries to see if E-Teams are the prime catalysts for change in men.

Second, the surveys used in the evaluations of the men's ministry of First Baptist Church were original. Sample surveys for men from other churches or parachurch organizations would be helpful. It would be a good study to see what men's ministries across the country have developed to assess the needs of their men.

Third, it would be helpful to study the impact of men's E-Teams compared to the impact of small groups composed of both men and women. Are the two different types of small groups equal in their impact on men? Or does the E-Team composed only of men have the greater impact? Or do both types help men but in different ways?

Fourth, in developing the men's ministry, the ideas for special events were original with the men's committee. A resource book composed of effective programming that other men's groups are doing would be very helpful. A good study would be to contact other churches with men's groups, asking them to list five of their most successful events.

Fifth, getting surveys back is difficult. Returns ran between approximately 35-40 percent. It would be helpful to know what other churches have done to generate a greater response.

Sixth, since other ministries warrant full-time ministers, it only makes good sense that men's ministries would also need full-time men, whose unique calling would be to build the men of the church through an organized, integrated program. The feasibility of Ministers of Men, or combinations such as Ministers of Men and Youth, or Ministers of Men and Missions, or Ministers of Men and Worship, or Ministers of Men and Visitation, needs further study. A study of what other churches are doing in this area would be beneficial.

Seventh, surveys were used to measure the spirituality of the men of First Baptist Church and the effectiveness of the program that was developed. The possibility of using personal interviews as an alternative measuring tool needs to be researched. The advantage of the personal interview would be in selecting the men to be interviewed. This could result in a survey that would be more accurate, because it would be more representative. For example, men could be interviewed according to age, education, type of employment, number of children, marital status, or other variables. Political polls operate on the principle of selective polling and are usually very accurate. Of course, random interviews could still be done.

Eighth, there is a need to research the possibility of using a test group. Give the same survey to three different groups: those not involved in the men's ministry, those moderately involved in the men's ministry, and those extensively involved in the men's ministry. This would provide a good basis of comparison. If the test group (those extensively involved in the program) did significantly better than the group not involved at all, this would point to the strength of the program.

Ninth, the possibility of variables in evaluating surveys needs to be studied. Men brought up in homes where fathers provided a good example for them might do better on surveys, regardless of a men's program. Also, the length a man has been a Christian may enter into how well he does on a survey.

Tenth, a final recommended area for further study would be the possibility of specialized training in men's ministry. Are theological schools offering significant training in this area? Are there seminaries that offer men's ministries as a specialized tract of study? Could a man get a D. Min. in men's ministry?

CHAPTER EIGHT

# HOW TO START A MEN'S MINISTRY

**Create Interest**

We began by building some activities that would appeal to men. We held a Dad/Lad breakfast at a local restaurant, using a hobby theme. The invitation produced things like remote control model airplanes, woodcarvings, and rare coin collections.

We also planned a pizza buffet around a fishing theme. An expert fisherman who was a Christian gave a talk on fishing. He testified that he himself had been caught and made a fisher of men. These activities created the initial interest.

**Develop Momentum**

Using videotapes, we held a Dad the Family Shepherd conference. To get the tapes, write to Dad the Family Shepherd, P.O. Box 21445, Little Rock, Arkansas 72221. Nine sessions were held, each led by gifted speakers. Outlines of the presentations, plus fill in the blanks and meaningful questions, were contained in attractive workbooks. Each man present received a workbook. We found these conference materials to be of the highest quality.

To show the videotapes, we rented a video projector from a nearby college. You could use a big-screen television if your group is small.

Later we participated in a live Dad the Family Shepherd conference with area churches. We felt the video conference had the most impact on our men, however. It motivated and launched our men's ministry. God used it to energize a hunger for men's ministries in the hearts of many men in our church.

As the interest in an effective men's ministry grew, we began to hear of the Promise Keepers movement. If you desire to do so, you can contact Promise Keepers by writing to them at P.O. Box 103001, Denver, Colorado 80250-3001.

When a Promise Keepers rally was held in Indianapolis, our men were primed for it. Sixty thousand men from across Indiana packed the Hoosier Dome for that first gathering. The men of our church were deeply stirred by the convicting messages. They also were deeply stirred by the unique experience of singing songs of worship and praise with thousands of other exuberant men.

Through the Dad the Family Shepherd conference (small) and the Promise Keepers conference (large), we developed sufficient momentum to get an ongoing men's program off the ground in our church.

## Build The Program

In both of those conferences, the challenge went forth to form small groups of men for the purpose of encouraging one another and holding one another accountable for growth and challenge. Because the interest was there, we seized the opportunity to form our first small men's group. We called it the E-Team, or encouragement team. We began with five men who met in a local restaurant every other Saturday for breakfast, fellowship, and Bible study. The E-Team members began to testify of changes they were making in their lives.

God used the E-Team to challenge me about the value of male friendships. I looked up a close friend of thirty years before. If I had not been in the small men's group, I never would have made the effort to reconnect with my old friend.

It is amazing how motivating a group of men can be. No one wants to come back to his group and say, "I didn't do what I said I was going to do." Just the thought of being accountable to your group will motivate you to follow through on your commitments.

When we cosponsored a live Dad the Family Shepherd conference with several area churches, our men were again challenged to get into a small group. The moment was right to establish a second E-Team. This group also consisted of five men and had the same format and purposes as the first E-Team.

In order to further build the program, we formed a men's committee to guide and maintain the men's ministry. This committee consisted of six men who each agreed to serve a two-year term. According to the committee's written statement of purpose, "The purpose of the men's ministry at First Baptist church is to provide the SON for every man in the church. 'S' stands for 'salvation.' 'O' stands for 'other men.' 'N' stands for 'nurture.'"

Not only did the purpose statement guide us; we also had a diagnostic test. We compiled a survey consisting of forty questions, all of which were designed to reveal the needs of our men. We sent the questionnaire to every man in our church, regardless of age. It was crafted to be anonymous.

From the responses, we were able to see many areas of special need. On the basis of these needs, we planned study materials for the E-Teams. We also planned special events and activities that would help meet the individual needs of the men of our church.

If you decide to build a men's ministry in your church, I suggest that you avoid merely planning activities that are typical of programs for men. Instead, take the time to discover the special needs of your own men; then structure your program to meet those definite needs. Our diagnostic test allowed many special needs to surface. You should plan on using some type of survey to help you find the pulse of the men God has placed in your church.

For example, the diagnostic test we used revealed that one of the major needs of our men was the need to get to know each other better. We began to meet this need by enlarging our ministry beyond the E-Team and men's committee levels. Here are some of the basics of the wider men's ministry that we put together.

We took a new look at our men's softball team, which actually predated the men's ministry. In light of our purpose statement to provide the SON for every man in the church ("o" stands for "other men"), however, we began to see the softball teams as more than recreation. Playing softball was an opportunity to get to know other men in the church. As the pastor, I began to promote the team. I came to see it as a valid part of our men's ministry.

We established an annual golf tournament. Although this event was also open to women and children, it still gave men an opportunity to invite unsaved friends and get to know other men in the church.

Following the golf tournament, we gave out prizes to those who participated. This high-profile recognition made the golf outing extra special.

We had father/child outings. We promoted, and encouraged fathers to take advantage of professional sports games as opportunities to do something enjoyable with their children. We attended these games as a group, and there usually was a very good turnout.

We had service projects. One year we painted a widow's house. This project not only was a blessing to the widow; it also was a great testimony to her neighbors and a bonding time for our men.

We put on widower-support luncheons. Some of the loneliest people in the body of Christ are men who have lost their wives. A couple times a year we invited all our widowers to a lunch. Being able to share their pains and struggles with one another meant a great deal to them.

We set up a pastor's prayer team consisting of seven people. Their responsibility was to pray for me on a specific day of the week. My job was to regularly give them my top seven requests and updates on the previous seven requests. Interceding for the pastor is a significant way for men to lead the church in prayer. Six of the seven people on my prayer team were men.

We also had an event to honor women. The men of the church planned and cooked a fabulous meal for all the women. The men financed it, and it was free for every woman of our church. The men served the meal, provided the program, and cleaned up afterward.

The women thoroughly enjoyed the meal, but the men benefited the most by serving together. As Jeff Samsel said, "Service unites us by bringing about a singularity of purpose" (*New Man*, March/April 1996).

We scheduled men's breakfasts to be held in a local restaurant. We encouraged men to invite their friends and sons to a buffet breakfast. We kept the program brief so that the men could still spend most of the day with their families.

At one breakfast we asked several men to share something that had really worked in their marriage or in their families.

We began circulating a men's newsletter. Instead of making this up ourselves, we made arrangements with *Men's Life*, 2850 Kalamazoo Avenue SE, Grand Rapids, Michigan 49560, to send every man in our church their quarterly newsletter. We found this loaded with helpful articles and challenging thoughts for men. The regular arrival of this newsletter served as a reminder and encourager to our men to be the kind of men God wants them to be.

### Sustain The Momentum

Men's programs have a tendency to wind down. Along with your regular program for men, you need to include something big and special at least once a year. Attending a Promise Keepers rally could be one of those momentum builders. It is the Super Bowl of men's ministries. Other possibilities could include a men's retreat, a father/son or father/daughter banquet, or a family life conference.

Every men's ministry needs a shot in the arm at regular intervals. Big and special events help renew interest in and create excitement about the total men's program. They also can be key opportunities to promote other facets of the men's program.

Finally, there are two things to keep in mind. First, recognize that E-Teams (small men's groups) are absolutely vital. Most growth in your men will occur in the context of a small group.

A part of Ron Rand's ministry for men has been squads –men divided up into small groups. Commenting on these squads, Rand said, "The amazing ability of the men to care for each other, bear each other's burdens and share those things of the heart has inspired the ministry beyond any other activity" (*For Fathers Who Aren't in Heaven*, Regal).

Second, recognize that your men's ministry does not have to be big to be effective. A men's ministry is good leaven that can leaven the whole church. As men grow stronger in their leadership roles, their influence will increase. Jesus' small group of men grew and eventually affected the whole church; so can the men's ministry in your local church.

* Adapted from the writer's article *"How To Build A Men's Ministry."* The Gospel Herald and Sunday School Times, pp 62-63, Fall 2001. Reprinted by permission of The Incorporated Trustees of the Gospel Worker Society and Union Gospel Press, PO Box 6059, Cleveland, OH 44101

# APPENDIX A

# CIRCLE OF NEEDS

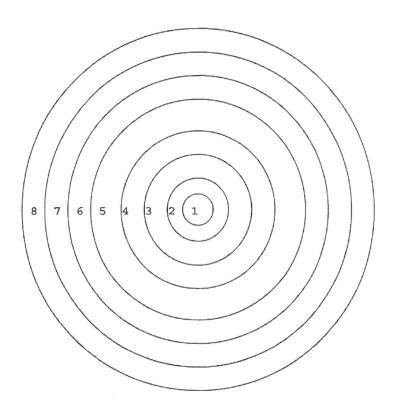

1. Walk with Christ
2. Personal Vision
3. Good Family Man
4. Church Involvement
5. Small Group - Being Mentored
6. Job Contentment
7. Mentoring Others
8. Balance

## APPENDIX B

## ACCOUNTABILITY QUESTIONS FOR MEN'S SMALL GROUPS

1. How much time did you spend in prayer this week?

2. Did you pray for the others in this group?

3. Did you put yourself in an awkward situation with a woman?

4. At anytime did you compromise your integrity?

5. What one sin plagued your walk with God this week?

6. Did you accomplish your spiritual goals this week?

7. Are you giving to the Lord's work financially?

8. How have you demonstrated a servant's heart?

9. Do you treat your peers and co-workers as people loved by God?

10. What was your biggest disappointment? How did you handle it?

11. What was your biggest joy? Did you thank God?

12. What do you see as your number one need for next week?

13. Are you satisfied with the time you spent with the Lord this week?

14. Did you take time to show compassion for others in need?

15. Did you control your tongue?

16. What did you do this week to enhance your relationship with your spouse?

17. Did you pray and read God's Word this week? What did you derive from this time?

18. In what ways have you launched out in faith since we last met?

19. In what ways has God blessed you this week? And what disappointments consumed your growth life this week?

20. Did you look at a woman in the wrong way?

21. Have you been tempted this week? How did you respond?

22. How has your relationship with Christ been changing?

23. Did you worship in church this week?

24. Have you shared your faith this week? How?

25. What are you wrestling with in your thought life?

26. What have you done for someone else this week?

27. Are the "visible" you and the "real" you consistent in this relationship?

(copied from Richardson, 1993, pp.50, 51)

# APPENDIX C

# KEYS TO JOB SATISFACTION

1. You are to see yourself as a servant to co-workers and customers.

   *For even the Son of Man did not come to be served, but to serve, and to give His life a ransom for many.*

   *-Mark 10:45*

2. You are to work with a motive of serving Christ, not men. Your work is an act of worship!

   *Slaves, be obedient to those who are your masters according to the flesh, with fear and trembling, in the sincerity of your heart, as to Christ; not by the way of eyeservice, as men-pleasers, but as slaves of Christ, doing the will of God from the heart. With good will render service, as to the Lord, and not to men.*

   *-Ephesians 6:5-7*

3. You are to have a healthy balance of work and leisure – not being lazy and not being a workaholic.

   *The fool folds his hands and consumes his own flesh. One hand full of rest is better than two fists of labor and striving after wind.*

   *-Ecclesiastes 4:5,6*

4. You are to autograph your work with excellence of effort.

   *Whatever you do, do your work heartily, as for the*

*Lord rather than for men;*

*-Colossians 3:23*

5. You are to maintain a high level of ethical distinction in your attitudes and actions on the job. Your character, your values, and your attitude should be so unique, so Christlike, that co-workers should stand amazed.

   *...that you may prove yourselves to be blameless and innocent, children of God above reproach in the midst of a crooked and perverse generation, among whom you appear as lights in the world, holding fast the word of life, so that in the day of Christ I may have cause to glory because I did not run in vain nor toil in vain.*

   *-Philippians 2:15,16*

6. You are to share the gospel with co-workers.

   *And He said to them, "Go into all the world and preach the gospel to all creation."*

   *-Mark 16:15*

7. You are to pursue peaceful relationships with co-workers as much as possible without violating your integrity.

   *Pursue after peace with all men, and after the sanctification without which no one will see the Lord.*

   *-Hebrews 12:14*

8. You are to cultivate a sense of gratitude and fulfillment in your work as a gift from God to bring glory to Him.

*I know that there is nothing better for them than to rejoice and to do good in one's lifetime, moreover, that every man who eats and drinks sees good in all his labor – it is the gift of God.*

-Ecclesiastes 3:12,13

9. You are to encourage other Christians toward discipleship.

*And we proclaim Him, admonishing every man and teaching every man with all wisdom, that we may present every man complete in Christ. And for this purpose also I labor, striving according to His power, which mightily works within me.*

-Colossians 1:28,29

10. You are to be content with your wages and not long for great wealth.

*And if we have food and covering, with these we shall be content. But those who want to get rich fall into temptation and a snare and many foolish and harmful desires which plunge men into ruin and destruction. For the love of money is a root of all sorts of evil, and some by longing for it have wandered away from the faith, and pierced themselves with many a pang.*

-I Timothy 6:8-10

11. You are to submit to your boss and to the rules of your company, with a good attitude.

*Urge bondslaves to be subject to their own masters in everything, to be well pleasing, not argumentative, not pilfering, but showing all good faith that they may adorn the doctrine of God our Savior in every respect.*

-Titus 2:9,10

*Servants, be submissive to your masters with all respect, not only to those who are good and gentle, but also to those who are unreasonable.*

-I Peter 2:18

- copied from *Your Work Matters To God* work book, Sherman, 1989, pp. 51-54
- Scripture references from NASV

## APPENDIX D

## UNITED STATES APPRENTICE CERTIFICATE

**The United States Department of Labor**

**Bureau of Apprenticeship and Training**
**Certificate of Completion of Apprenticeship**

This is to certify that

STEVEN D. FEICK

has completed an apprenticeship for the occupation

MOLD MAKER

under the sponsorship of

ADMAR MOLD & ENGINEERING, INC.

in accordance with the basic standards of apprenticeship established by the Secretary of Labor

OCTOBER 4, 1989

## APPENDIX E

## THE DIAGNOSTIC TEST

Dear Brother in Christ,

We rejoice in your involvement in the ministry of First Baptist Church. Recently a Men's Ministry Committee was formed to oversee an ongoing men's program at First Baptist. In order to plan a growing and more effective ministry to men, we need to know where you are as a man. Enclosed is a simple diagnostic test, which will help us to determine the needs of men in the church. Please help us by completing it and returning it in the self-addressed envelope by February 28th. Be sure to use your pin number (see instructions). Please answer the questions honestly. Your test will be anonymous.

Instructions for diagnostic test:

1. Skip all questions that do not apply to you.

2. Your PIN number is the year of your birth, plus the last four digits of your social security number.

Example:

    1959 – year of birth

    6655 – last four digits of Social Security Number.

    8614 = PIN number

By using the PIN number, your test will remain anonymous. Any future tests will ask for the same PIN number, making it possible to measure progress and the effectiveness of our program.
Thank you in advance for your cooperation.

Prayerfully Yours,
The Men's Committee

Joe Banks

Vern Fredericks

Bob Hatfield

Mike Potts

Roger Smith

Pastor Karl

P.S. This test will take you approximately 15-20 minutes to complete.

## Diagnostic Test for Men in the 90s

Number_____ Date of Test_____

1. Do you presently have a quiet time (a time of Bible reading and prayer) at least once a week?

2. Do you presently have a quiet time at least three times a week?

3. Do you have a sense that you are growing in your Christian life?

4. Would you describe your growth in the last year as (circle one) non-existent, meager, slow but steady, sporadic, abundant?

5. Would you describe your thought life as sexually pure with occasional spots, or often contaminated by impure thoughts, or somewhere in between?

6. Circle the one that is most true? I never, very seldom, often, witness for Christ to others.

7. T or F – I have some weaknesses that I need to get victory over in my life.

8. T or F – I have gotten victory over at least one weak area in the last year.

9. T or F – My passion in life is to be the man God wants me to be in my family, in my church, in my job, and in my community.

10. T or F – I am bored with my Christian life.

11. T or F – I am enjoying my Christian life.

12. T or F – I am excited about my Christian life.

13. On a scale of 1-10, (10 representing the ideal), how would you score your marriage?

14. Have you made any changes to improve your marriage in the last year?

15. T or F – I sense that my wife values my leadership in the home.

16. Circle one: I never, seldom, often, say romantic things to my wife.

17. When it comes to spending effective time with your kids, score yourself from 1-10 (10 representing the ideal).

18. Circle one: I am encouraged, discouraged, as a husband and father.

19. Are you part of a men's small group that meets on a regular basis?

20. Do you have any close male friends?

21. Have you grown close to any other men in the church in the last year?

22. T or F - I regularly receive encouragement from other men.

23. I regularly seek to encourage other men in their walk with God and family responsibilities.

24. T or F – I regularly attend one church service a week. (Church service would be a.m. or p.m. worship service, a Sunday school class, or Wednesday night prayer service.)

25. T or F – I regularly attend two church services a week.

26. T or F – I regularly attend three church services a week.

27. T or F – I have committed myself to at least one job in my church.

28. Circle one: I give less than 5% of my salary to God each year, at least 5%, or 10% or more.

29. T or F – I live a consistent Christian life at work.

30. T or F - I am enjoying contentment in my present job.

31. T or F – I am frustrated in my present job.

32. T or F - I am excited about my future in secular work.

33. I am presently being mentored by another man. (Mentoring is a regular and deliberate building into another man's life.)

34. T or F - I am presently mentoring another man.

35. T or F – I believe I have a vision of what God wants to accomplish through my life.

36. On a scale of 1-10 (10 representing the ideal), rate how well you are maintaining the right kind of priorities.

37. On a scale of 1-10 (10 representing the ideal), rate the impact that the men's program of First Baptist Church has had on your life. The men's ministry of First Baptist presently consists of two small groups (E-Teams); an early morning prayer meeting; special events such as Promise Keepers, Dad the Family Shepherd, and sports activities; all opportunities to be trained to do ministry or be the man God wants you to be in your marriage, family, and job; and all opportunities to form friendships with other men.

38. On a scale of 1-10 (10 representing the ideal), rate the impact that the preaching from the pulpit has had on your walk with God and effectiveness as a husband and father.

39. On a scale of 1-10 (10 representing the ideal), rate the impact that the Sunday School program has had.

40. What do you feel are your two greatest needs at this time in your life?

# APPENDIX F

# DIAGNOSTIC TEST RESULTS

| Questions 1 & 2 | Frequency of quiet time | 3 times a week or more | 71% |
|---|---|---|---|
| | | 1 or 2 times a week | 29% |
| Questions 3 | Growing Spiritually | Yes | 81% |
| | | No | 19% |
| Questions 4 | Kind of Spiritual Growth | Slow/Steady | 58% |
| | | Abundant | 12% |
| | | Sporadic | 15% |
| | | Non-existent | 4% |
| Question 5 | Purity of Thought Life | Occasional Thoughts of Impurity | 44% |
| | | Often Thoughts of Impurity | 16% |
| | | In Between Occasional and Often | 40% |
| Question 6 | Witnessing | Often | 33% |
| | | Seldom | 8% |
| | | Never | 58% |
| Question 7 | Have Weaknesses | True | 96% |
| Question 8 | Victory over one weak area in last year | True | 71% |
| | | False | 29% |
| Question 9 | Passion to be man God wants | True | 100% |
| Question 10 | Bored with Christian life | True | 8% |
| | | False | 92% |
| Question 11 | Enjoying Christian life | True | 92% |
| | | False | 8% |
| Question 12 | Excited about your Christian life | True | 77% |
| | | False | 23% |

| Question 13 | Score your marriage | 1-10 | 7.6 |
| --- | --- | --- | --- |
| Question 14 | Changes in marriage in last year | True | 88% |
| | | False | 12% |
| Question 15 | Wife values your leadership | True | 95% |
| Question 16 | Say romantic things to wife | Often | 65% |
| | | Seldom | 35% |
| Question 17 | Spend effective time with kids | 1-10 | 6.4 |
| Question 18 | Encouraged as husband and Father | True | 90% |
| | | False | 10% |
| Question 19 | In a small group | True | 15% |
| | | False | 85% |
| Question 20 | Close male friends | True | 69% |
| | | False | 31% |
| Question 21 | Grew close to other men in church last year | True | 54% |
| | | False | 46% |
| Question 22 | Regularly receive encouragement from other men | True | 62% |
| | | False | 38% |
| Question 23 | Regularly encourages other men | True | 66% |
| | | False | 34% |
| Question 24-26 | Attending church services | 1 service a week | 16% |
| | | 2 services a week | 42% |
| | | 3 services a week | 42% |
| Question 27 | At least one job in church | True | 64% |
| | | False | 35% |
| Question 28 | Giving | Less then 5% | 12% |
| | | 5% or more | 35% |
| | | 10% or more | 52% |

| Question 29 | Consistent Christian life at work | True | 82% |
| --- | --- | --- | --- |
| | | False | 18% |
| Question 30 | Contentment with job | True | 70% |
| | | False | 30% |
| Question 31 | Frustrated with job | True | 32% |
| | | False | 68% |
| Question 32 | Excited about job in secular work | True | 53% |
| | | False | 47% |
| Question 33 | Being mentored | True | 5% |
| | | False | 95% |
| Question 34 | Mentoring others | True | 12% |
| | | False | 82% |
| Question 35 | Have a vision | True | 64% |
| | | False | 36% |
| Question 36 | Maintain priorities-balance | 1-10 | 6.9 |
| Question 37 | Impact of men's ministry on your life | 1-10 | 5.1 |
| Question 38 | Impact of preaching | 1-10 | 8 |
| Question 39 | Impact of Sunday School | 1-10 | 7.2 |

# APPENDIX G

# FELT NEEDS TABULATIONS

> PERSONAL WALK WITH GOD - 11

> VISION - 0

> GOOD FAMILY MAN - 15

> CHURCH INVOLVEMENT - 6

> SMALL GROUPS - 2
> MALE FRIENDS - 2

> MENTORING - 0

> JOB SATISFACTION - 3

> BALANCE - 4

# APPENDIX H

# THE MISSION OF THE MEN'S MINISTRY OF FIRST BAPTIST

```
             Salvation

             Other men

             Nurture

             *encouragement
             *challenge
             *accountability
             *burden bearing
             *mentoring
             *equipping
             *correcting
```

compare #5,6 of circle

```
             walking
             with God

             leading their
             families

             building
             their church

             making a
             living

             having a
             testimony in
             the world
```

compare #1,2, 3,4,7,8 of circle

CIRCLE OF NEEDS

1. Walking With God
2. Vision
3. Good Family Man
4. Involvement In Church
5. Small Group
6. Mentoring
7. Job Satisfaction
8. Balance

# APPENDIX I

## PROMISE KEEPERS SURVEY

1. I was enriched by the music and worship of the conference. <u>8.75</u>

2. I was encouraged spiritually by the large gathering of men hungry for God. <u>9.5</u>

3. I was challenged by the messages of the speakers. <u>8.75</u>

4. I was encouraged by the fellowship of the men I came with to the conference. <u>9.5</u>

5. I appreciated the opportunity to make friends with the men I came with to the conference. <u>10</u>

## FATHER/CHILD OUTINGS SURVEY

Please circle using 1 being low and 5 being high.

> The Father/Child Outings have given me an opportunity to spend quality time with my children.
> (1 2 3 4 5) <u>3.8</u>

> The Father/Child Outings have been helpful to me in getting to know other men. (1 2 3 4 5) <u>3.8</u>

Please give us a suggestion for a possible Father/Child Outing for the future.

## APPENDIX J

## FOLLOW-UP QUESTIONNAIRE

Dear Brother in Christ,

Greetings in our dear Savior's name. We hope you are excited about being the man God wants you to be. Previously, we sent out a diagnostic test and received a good percentage back. Thank you. On the basis of that test, the men's committee has developed a number of ministries and events designed to meet the primary needs reflected in the test. This questionnaire is a follow-up to see if the things we have been doing are helping to meet your needs as a man. Please fill it out according to the instructions.

The men's ministry, in recent days, has consisted of a live Dad the Family Shepherd conference, a Friendship Evangelism seminar, Promise Keepers conferences, a Man of His Word Video series, Father/Child outings (i.e., Wizard games), and golf outings. Other components would include men's softball, E-Teams, men's breakfasts, serving on the men's committee, serving on Pastor Karl's prayer support team, widower's support luncheons, special workdays at the church, and work projects, such as painting a widow's house.

Please check appropriate box.

☐ I have not been involved in any of the men's ministries. (If you check this box, answer questions 9 and 10 only and return.)

☐ I have occasionally been involved in men's ministries. (If you check this box, answer all the questions and return.)

☐ I have often been involved in men's ministries. (If you checked this box, answer all the questions and return.)

This questionnaire is designed to be anonymous. Please add the last four numbers of your social security number plus your year of birth. The total is your PIN #. Put your PIN # on the line marked PIN #. Example:

    7712 – last four digits of S. S. #
    <u>1951</u> – year of birth
    9663 – total = PIN number
    PIN #_____

Sincerely,
The Men's Committee of First Baptist Church

## Men's Ministry Follow-Up Questionnaire

1. I have been able to meet and get to know other men through the men's ministries of First Baptist Church. T or F.
2. Through the men's ministries of First Baptist Church, God has created in me a greater awareness of my needs as a man. T or F.
3. On a scale of 1-10 (With one being a low score and ten a high score) measure the impact of the men's ministry of First Baptist Church on your desire to grow into the man God wants you to be.
4. Through involvement in the men's ministry, I made this definite change in my life _____
   _____.
   (Leave blank if no change can be recalled.)
5. One particular event sponsored by the men's ministry that was very helpful to me was _____
   _____.
   (If there were more than one, please list.)
6. I have invited unchurched friends to men's activities. T or F. At least one came. T or F.

7. Through men's ministries of First Baptist church, I feel I have become a better husband. T or F.

8. Through men's ministries of First Baptist Church I feel I have become a better father. T or F.

9. I believe I have a healthy contentment with my job. T or F.

10. I am growing in my boldness to witness to people at work. T or F.

11. Involvement in men's ministries of the church is helping me to cope with the pressure of my job. T or F.

12. On a scale of 1-10 measure the encouragement that men's ministries of First Baptist Church has had on your life.

**Please return both pages by March 3.**

# APPENDIX K

# RESPONSES TO THE FOLLOW-UP QUESTIONNAIRE

| | | | | |
|---|---|---|---|---|
| Small Groups | Getting to know other men through men's ministry of First Baptist Church | Involved often 9 - yes | Involved Occasionally 4 - yes | 93% Yes |
| Vision | Through men's ministry God has created in me a greater awareness of my needs as a man. | 7 -yes | 4 - yes 3 - no | 79% Yes |
| Vision | Scale of 1-10 measure the impact of men's ministry on your desire to grow into the man God wants you to be | 8.1 | 5.2 | Combined Average 6.9 |
| Walk with God | I have invited unchurched friends to men's activities | 3 - no 5 - yes | 6 - no | 36% Yes |
| Good Family Man | Through men's ministry I feel I have become a better husband | 7 - yes 1 - no | 4 - yes 2 - no | 79% Yes |
| Good Family Man | Through men's ministry I feel I have become a better father | 7 - yes 1 - no | 3 - yes 2 - no | 79% Yes |
| Job Satisfaction | Healthy contentment with Job | 6 - yes 2 - no | 5 - yes 1 - no | 79% Yes |
| Walk with God | Growing in boldness to witness at work | 7 - yes 1 - no | 3 - yes 2 - no | 77% Yes |
| Job Satisfaction | Involvement in men's ministries is helping me cope with job pressures | 8 - yes | 2 - yes 4 - no | 71% Yes |
| Encompasses all 8 needs | Scale of 1-10 measure encouragement men's ministry has had on your life | 8.0 | 4.0 | Combined Average 6.5 |

# BIBLIOGRAPHY

Alford, Henry. 1958. *Alford's Greek Testament,* Vol. 3. Chicago, IL: Moody Press.

Amneus, Daniel. 1979. *Back To Patriarchy.* New Rochelle, NY: Arlington House.

Anders, Max. 1997. *The Church.* TN: Nelson Publishers.

Arndt, William, F. and Gingrich, F. Wilbur. 1957. *A Greek English Lexicon of the New Testament.* Chicago, IL: University of Chicago Press.

Balswick, Jack. 1992. *Men At The Crossroads.* Downers Grove, IL: InterVarsity Press.

Barclay, William. 1975. *Letters to Galatians and Ephesians.* Westminister, MD: John Karp Press.

Barker, Kenneth L. and Kohlenberger III, John,(Eds). 1994. *Zondervan NIV Bible Commentary,* Vol. 1&2. Winona Lake, IN: BMH Books.

Barna, George and McKay, William Paul. 1984. *Vital Signs.* Wheaton, IL: Crossway Books.

Barna, George. 1993. *The Future of the American Family.* Chicago, IL: Moody Press.

Barna, George. 1998. *The Second Coming of the Church.* Waco, TX: Word Publishers.

Baron, Bruce, 1990. *Putting Women in Their Place: 1 Timothy 2 and Evangelical Views of Women in Church Leadership.* In Ron Youngblood (Ed), *Journal of the Evangelical Theological Society* (pp. 46-57), Vol. 33, No.4, Dec. Jackson, MS: Evangelical Theological Society.

Bauer, Gary. 1992. *Our Journey Home.* Dallas, TX: Word Publishing.

Bilezikian, Gilbert. 1985. *Beyond Sex Roles.* Grand Rapids, MI: Baker Books.

Bilezikian, Gilbert. 1987. *Hierarchist and Egalitarian Inculturations.* In Ron Youngblood (Ed) *Journal of the Evangelical Theological Society* (pp. 421-426), Vol 30, No.4, Dec. Jackson, MS: Evangelical Theological Society.

Blankenhorn, David. 1995. *Fatherless America.* New York, NY: Basic Books.

Bly, Robert. 1992. *Iron John.* New York, NY: Random House.

Boice, James. 1997. *An Expositional Commentary On Ephesians.* Grand Rapids, MI: Baker Books.

Borland, James. 1991. *Women in the Life and Teaching of Jesus.* In John Piper and Wayne Grudem (Eds) *Recovering Biblical Manhood and Womanhood* (pp. 113-123). Wheaton, IL: Crossway Books.

Bounds, E.M. 1961. *A Treasury of Prayer.* Minneapolis, MN: Bethany House.

Brauch, Manfred T., Bruce, F. F., Davids, Peter H., and Kaiser Jr., Walter C. 1996. *Hard Sayings of the Bible.* Downers Grove, IL: InterVarsity Press.

Brown, David., Fausset, A. R., and Jamieson, Robert. 1982. *Commentary On the Whole Bible.* Grand Rapids, MI: Zondervan.

Cole, Edwin. 1982. *Maximized Manhood.* New Kensington, Pa: Whitaker House.

Collins, Gary. 1995. *Family Shock.* Wheaton, IL: Tyndale House.

Colson, Charles. 1978. *The Body.* Dallas, TX: Word Publishers.

Cook, Robert. 1978. *In Step With God.* Chappaqua, NY: Christian Herald Association.

Culver, Robert. 1989. in Bonnedell Clouse and Robert Clouse (Eds), *Women In Ministry.* Downers Grove, IL: InterVarsity.

Davies, Richard. 1984. *Handbook for Doctor of Ministry Projects.* Lanham, MD: University Press of America.

Dana, H. E. and Mantey, Julius R. 1927. *A Manual Grammar of the Greek New Testament.* New York, NY: The Macmillan Company.

Delitzsch, F. and Keil, C.F. 1971. *Biblical Commentary on the Old Testament,* Vol. 1. Grand rapids, MI: Eerdmans.

Dorman, Jim. and Maxwell, John. 1997. *Becoming a Person of Influence.* Nashville, TN: Nelson.

Ellicott, Charles J. 1883. *The Pastoral Epistles of St. Paul.* London, England: Longmans, Green, and Co.

Elliot, Elisabeth. 1992. *Discovering Joy Through Discipline,* Chapter Five, The Discipline of Time. Lincoln, NE: Back to the Bible.

Engstrom, Ted W. 1989. *The Fine Art of Mentoring.* Brentwood, TN: Wolgemuth and Hyatt.

Farrar, Steve. 1990. *Point Man.* Sisters, OR: Multnomah, division of Questar.

Foh, Susan. 1989. In Bonnedell Clouse and Robert Clouse (Eds) *Women in Ministry.* Downers Grove, IL: InterVarsity.

Foulkes, Francis. 1963. *The Epistle of Paul to the Ephesians.* In R. V. Tasker (Ed), *Tyndale New Testament Commentaries.* Grand Rapids, MI: Eerdmans.

Gaebelein, Frank E. 1978. *The Expositor's Bible Commentary,* Vol. II (Ed). Grand Rapids, MI: Zondervan.

Gangel, Kenn and Betty. 1992. *Growing in Grace and Godliness.* Denver, CO: Accent Publishers.

Ghant, Rick. 1993. *Five Myths of Male Sexuality.* Chicago, IL: Moody Press.

Glenn, Norval D. 1996. *Values, Attitudes and the State of the American Marriage.* In David Popenoe (Ed), *Promises to Keep: Decline and Renewal of Marriage in America.* Lanham, MD: Rowman and Littlefield.

Gorsuch, Geoff and Schaffer, Dan. 1994. *Brother!* Colorado Springs: CO: Navpress.

Gromacki, Robert. 1977. *Called to Be Saints.* Shaumburg, IL: Regular Baptist Press.

Grosheide, F.W. 1953. *Commentary on First Corinthians, New International Commentary on the New Testament.* Grand Rapids, MI: Eerdmans.

Grudem, Wayne. 1987. *Prophecy-Yes, But Teaching-No: Paul's Consistent Advocacy of Women's Participation Without Governing Authority.* In Ronald Youngblood (Ed), pp. 11-23. The Journal of the Evangelical Society, Vol. 30, No. 1.

Grudem, Wayne. 1991. *The Meaning of "Kephale" ("Head"): A Response to Recent Studies.* In John Piper and Wayne Grudem *(Eds), Recovering Biblical Manhood and Womanhood* (pp. 425-468). Wheaton, IL: Crossing Books.

Grudem, Wayne. 1994. *Systematic Theology.* Grand Rapids, MI: Zondervan.

Guthrie, Donald. 1960. *The Pastoral Epistles.* Grand Rapids, Mich: Eerdmans.

Guthrie, Donald and Motyer, J. A. 1975. *The New Bible Commentary, Revised.* Grand Rapids, MI: Eerdmans.

Hanson, A. T. 1982. *The New Century Bible Commentary, The Pastoral Epistles.* Grand Rapids, MI: Eerdmans and Marshall.

Hardenbrook, Weldon. 1991. *Where's Dad?* In John Piper and Wayne Grudem (Eds), *Recovering Biblical Manhood and Womanhood* (pp. 378-387). Wheaton, IL: Crossway Books.

Harley, Willard, Jr. 1994. *His Needs Her Needs.* Grand Rapids, MI: Fleming H. Revell.

Harley, Willard, Jr. 1997. *Your Love and Marriage.* Grand Rapids, MI: Fleming H. Revell.

Harris, Robert, Archer, Gleason and Waltke, Bruce. 1980. *Theological Workbook of the Old Testament,* Volumes 1,2. Chicago, IL: Moody Press.

Harrison, Everett F. and Pfeiffer, Charles F. (Eds). 1973. *The Wycliffe Bible Commentary.* Chicago, IL: Moody Press.

Hendricks, Howard and Hendricks, William. 1995. *As Iron Sharpens Iron.* Chicago, IL: Moody Press.

Horn, Wade and Whitehead, Barbara D. 1998. *Fatherhood Facts,* 3rd Edition. Gaithersburg, MD: National Fatherhood Initiative.

Horner, Bob, Ralston, Ron, and Sunde, David. 1995. *Promise Builders.* Denver, CO: Promise Keepers.

Hodge, Charles. 1974. *First Epistle to the Corinthians.* Grand Rapids, MI: Eerdmans.

Hughes, Kent R. 1991. *Disciplines of a Godly Man.* Wheaton, IL: Crossway Books.

Hybels, Bill. 1998. *Too Busy Not To Pray.* Downers Grove, IL: InterVarsity Press.

Ironside, Harry. 1917. *Addresses on the First and Second Epistles of Timothy.* New York, NY: Loizeaux Brothers.

Jewett, Paul. 1975. *Man as Male and Female.* Grand Rapids, MI: Eerdmans.

Kent, Homer A. 1958. *The Pastoral Epistles.* Chicago, IL: Moody Press.

Kent, Homer A. 1971. *Ephesians-The Gory of the Church.* Chicago, IL: Moody Press.

Kent, Homer A. 1976. *The Freedom of God's Sons.* Grand Rapids, MI: Baker Books.

Knight, George W. 1984. *Authenteo in Reference to Women in 1 Tim 2:12. In New Testament Studies,* 30:154.

Knight, George W. 1992. *New International Greek Testament Commentary, Commentary on the Pastoral Epistles.* Grand Rapids, MI: Patermaster Press.

Kostenberger, Andreas J., Schreiner, Thomas K., and Baldwin, H. Scott. 1995. *Women in the Church.* Grand Rapids, MI: Baker Books.

Leedy, Paul. 1995. *Practical Research.* New York, NY: MacMillan.

Lewis, Robert and Hendricks, William. 1991. *Rocking the Roles.* Colorado, Springs, CO: Navpress.

Lewis, Robert and Campbell, Rich. 1995. *Real Family Values.* Gresham, OR: Vision House Publishers.

Liddell, Henry G. and Scott, Robert. 1968. *Greek-English Lexicon.* England: Oxford University Press.

Liefield, Walter. 1987. *Women and the Nature of Ministry.* In Ron Youngblood (Ed) Journal Of the Evangelical Theological Society. Jackson, MS: Evangelical Theological Society.

Liefield, Walter. 1989. In Bonnedell Clouse and Robert Clouse (Eds). *Women in Ministry.* Downers Grove, IL: InterVarsity Press.

Litfin, Duane. 1983. *1 Timothy. The Bible Knowledge Commentary.* Wheaton, IL: Victor Books.

MacDonald, Gordon. 1977. *The Effective Father.* Wheaton, Il:

Tyndale House.

MacGillis, Donald and ABC News. *Crime in America.* Radnor, PA: Chilton Books.

Maxwell, John. 1996. *Partners in Prayer.* Nashville, TN: Nelson Publishers.

Maxwell, Leslie E. 1987. *Women in Ministry.* Wheaton, IL: Victor Books.

McDowell, Josh and Hostetler, Bob. 1994. *Right from Wrong.* Dallas, TX: Word Publishers.

McDowell, Josh and Hostetler, Bob. 1998. *The New Tolerance.* Wheaton, IL: Tyndale Press.

McGill, Michael E. 1985. *The McGill Report on Male Intimacy* (pp. 157,158) as cited by Kent Hughes, p.60.

Mickelsen, Alvera. 1989. In Bonnedell Clouse and Robert Clouse (Eds), *Women in Ministry.* Downers Grove, IL: InterVarsity Press.

Mitchell, Daniel R. 1983. *1,2 Corinthians.* In Edward Hindson and Woodrow Kroll (Eds) *The Liberty Bible Commentary.* Nashville, TN: Nelson Publishers.

Moo, Douglas. 1991. *What Does It Mean Not to Teach or Have Authority Over Men?* In John Piper and Wayne Grudem (Eds), *Recovering Biblical Manhood and Womanhood* (pp. 179-193). Wheaton, IL: Crossway Books.

Mounce, William. 2000. *Word Biblical Commentary, Pastoral Epistles.* Nashville, TN: Nelson Publishers.

Neuer, Werner. 1991. *Man and Woman in Christian Perspective.*

Wheaton, IL: Crossway Books.

*New Illustrated Webster's Dictionary.* 1992. Chicago, IL: Ferguson Publishing Company.

Nicholas, David R. 1979. *What's a Woman to do...in the Church.* Scottsdale, AZ: Good Life Productions.

Nielsen, A. C. 1986. *Television.* Northbrook, IL: Nielson Report, as cited by Kent Hughes, p.74.

Oliver, Gary J. 1993. *Masculinity at the Crossroads.* Chicago, IL: Moody Press.

Ortlund, Raymond. 1991. *Male-Female Equality and Male Headship.* In John Piper and Wayne Grudem (Eds), *Recovering Biblical Manhood and Womanhood* (pp. 95-113). Wheaton, IL: Crossway Books.

Osterhaus, James. 1993. *Building Strong Male Relationships.* Chicago, IL: Moody Press.

Osterhaus, James. 1994. *Bonds of Iron.* Chicago, IL: Moody Press.

Patterson, James and Kim, Peter. 1991. *The Day America Told the Truth.* New York: NY: Prentice Hall, as cited by Kent Hughes, p. 139.

Pearsall, Paul. 1990. *The Power of the Family.* New York, NY: Doubleday.

Piper, John. 1991. *A Vision of Biblical Complementary.* In John Piper and Wayne Grudem (pp. 131-139), *Recovering Biblical Manhood and Womanhood.* Wheaton, IL: Crossway Books.

Popenoe, David and Whitehead, Barbara D. 1999. *The State of our*

Unions: *The Social Health of Marriage in America.* The National Marriage Project, Rutgers University.

Quinn, Jerome and Wacker, William. 2000. *First and Second Letters to Timothy.* Grand Rapids, MI: Eerdmans.

Radmacher, Earl (Ed). 1997. *The Nelson Study Bible.* Nashville, TN: Nelson Publishers.

Rand, Ron. 1986. *For Fathers Who Aren't in Heaven.* Ventura, CA: Regal.

Richardson, Pete. 1993. *Focusing Your Men's Ministry.* Boulder, CO: Promise Keepers.

Richardson, Pete. 1994. *Why Christian Men Need Each Other.* Chicago, IL: Moody Press.

Robertson, A. T. 1931. *Word Pictures in the New Testament,* Vol IV. Nashville, TN: Broadman Press.

Ryrie, Charles. 1970. *The Place of Women in the Church.* Chicago, IL: Moody Press.

Sanders, Oswald J. 1994. *Spiritual Leadership.* Chicgo, IL: Moody Press.

Saucy, Robert. 1972. *The Church in God's Program.* Chicago, IL: Moody Press.

Schlatter, A. 1914. *Die Korinthische Theologie.* In *Beitrage zur Forderung Chirislicher Theologie,* as cited in Neuer, p.20.

Sell, Charles. 1981. *Family Ministry.* Grand Rapids, MI: Zondervan Press.

Sell, Charles. 1996. *Power Dads.* Ann Arbor, MI: Servant

Publications.

Sherman, Doug. 1989. *Your Work Matters to God.* Garland, TX: Career Impact Ministries and E. Films and Videos.

Simpson, David. 1995. *It's Who You Know: Winning with People.* Gresham, OR: Vision House.

Smalley, Gary and Trent, John. 1992. *The Hidden Value of a Man.* Colorado Springs, CO: Focus on the Family Publishing.

Smalley, Gary and Trent, John. 1994. *Leaving the Light On.* Sisters, OR: Questar Publishers.

Smith, Bill. 1988. *Quiet Time.* Little Rock, AR: Quiet Time Ministries.

Sonderman, Steve. 1996. *How to Build a Life Changing Men's Ministry.* Minneapolis, MN: Bethany House Publishers.

Spencer, Aida B. 1985. *Beyond the Curse.* Nashville, TN: Nelson Press.

Stitzinger, Michael F. 1981. *Genesis 1-3 and the Male/Female Role Relationship.* In John C. Whitcomb (Ed), Grace Theological Journal. Winona Lake, IN: Grace Theological Seminary.

Swindoll, Charles. 1985. *Excellence in Ministry.* Fullerton, CA: Insight For Living Publishing.

Towner, Philip. 1994. *1,2 Timothy and Titus.* In Grant Osborne (Ed), *The NIV New Testament Commentary Series.* Downers Grove, IL: InterVarsity Press.

Von Rad, Gerhard. 1972. *Genesis: A Commentary,* Revised Edition. Philadelphia, PA: Westminster.

Vos, Clarence. 1968. *Women in O. T. Worship,* 18N25, as cited by Stitzinger, p. 32.

Wagner, Glenn E. and Dietrich Green. 1994. *Stategies for a Successful Marriage.* Colorado Springs, CO: NavPress.

Waltke, Bruce K. 1987, January – March. *1 Corinthians 11: 2-16: An Interpretation.* Bibliotheca Sacra. Dallas, TX: Dallas Theological Seminary.

Ward, Ronald A. 1974. *Commentary on 1,2 Timothy and Titus.* Waco, TX: Word Publishers.

Weber, Stu. 1993. *Tender Warrior.* Sisters, OR: Questar Publishing.

Wemp, Sumner. 1983. In Edward Hindson and Woodrow Kroll (Eds), *The Liberty Bible Commentary, 1,2 Timothy, Titus, Philemon.* Nashville, TN: Nelson Publishers.

Whitefield, George. 1832. *Sermons on Important Subjects.* London, England: Henry Fisher, Son, and P. Jackson Publishers.

Zuck, Roy. 1965, April. *Greek Words for "Teach".* Bibliotheca Sacra. Dallas, TX: Dallas Theological Seminary.

## PERIODICALS

Bechtle, Michael. (1995, May,June). How to balance priorities. *A New Man,* p.76.

Children need input of both mother and father. (1994, March 10). *USA Today.*

The church's sexual demographics. (1991, Winter). *Leadership,* pp. 16-20.

Dobson, James. (1999, November). Statistics on marriage and the family. *Family News*, Issue number 11, pp. 2-5.

Etter, Terry. (1994, September, October). Tips for a great men's group. *New Man*, pp. 51-53.

Etter, Terry (Ed). (1996, June). *Lifeline*, Men's Life Newsletter, Grand Rapids, MI.

Etter, Terry. (1997, Summer). The importance of male friendships. *Lifeline*, Men's Life Newsletter, Grand Rapids, MI.

Flexible Ethics – It Depends. (1997, April 29). *USA Today Snapshots*.

Forman, Roland, I. K. (1995, Spring). Mentoring tomorrow's leaders. *Kindred Spirit*, Vol. 19, No. 1, pp. 4-7.

Gilbreath, Edward. (1995, February 6). Manhood's great awakening-Promise Keepers. *Christianity Today,* pp. 21-26, 28.

Gregory, Richard. (1995, July, August). Issues in ministering to men. *Voice*, pp. 14,15.

Hedegaard, Erik. (1991, November). The men's movement is here. *McCall's*, pp. 98, 100, 209.

Helmbock, Thomas, A. (1996, Summer). Insights on Tolerance. *Cross and Cresent*, p.2.

Hoffer, Richard and Smith, Shelly. (1995, January 16). Putting his house in order. *Sports Illustrated.* pp. 26-32.

Horn, Wade, F. (1997, July, August). Absentee fathers. *Worship Leader,* p. 10.

House, Wayne, H. (1989, Summer). Caught in the middle. *Kindred*

*Spirit,* pp. 12-14.

Howard, Grant J. (1995, Fall). Balancing life's demands. *Kindred Spirit,* Vol. 19, No. 3.

Kelly, Dennis. (1996, January 17). Mentors show poor children the path to college. *USA Today,* p.6D.

McDowell, Josh. (1994, November). Help your teen make the right choice. *Focus on the Family,* pp. 3,4.

Miller, Calvin. (1996, March, April). Vision. *Worship Leader,* pp.28-33.

Minerbrook, Scott. (1995, February). Lives without father. *U.S. News and World Report,* pp. 50, 52, 54, 56.

Morley, Patrick. (1996-2000). *A Look in the Mirror,* Newsletter of Man in the Mirror Ministry, Nos. 17,24,41,47,52,65.

Morley, Patrick. (1999, July, August). Are you a priority male? *New Man,* p. 63.

Poverty-fathers and Welfare. (1994, December 12). *The Times Union,* Warsaw, IN, p.4A.

Robertson, Brian. (1994, March 14). The Value of the nuclear family. *Insight,* pp. 18-20.

Samsel, Jeff. (1996, March, April). Men at work-and play. *New Man,* p. 69.

Seger, Paul. (1996, January, February). Mentors. *Voice,* pp. 14,15.

Shapiro, Joseph, Schrof, Joannie, Tharp, Mike, and Friedman, Dorian. Honor thy children. *U. S. News & World Report,* pp. 39, 42, 27-49.

Strang, Stephen. (1998, September, October). Fizzle- proof your men's group. *New Man,* p. 34.

Swindoll, Charles. (1999). The Bible is his leader. *Better Families,* Vol. 22, No. 8.

Vincent, Lynn. (2000, November 11). Sexual purity of 4,000 active pastors. *World,* p.20.

Way, Warren S. (1996, May, June). The bigness trap. *Ministries Today,* p.47.

Weber, Stu. (1996, June). Someone to lean on. *Focus on the Family,* pp. 2-4.

Wuthnow, Robert. (1994, February 7). How small groups are transforming our lives. *Christianity Today,* pp. 21-24.

Yorkey, Mike and Jackson, Peb. (1992, June). Finding new friends on the block. *Focus on the Family,* pp. 2-4.

## NONPERIODICALS

Back to Men of Integrity Survey, 1999. Promise Keepers, Denver, CO.

Dad the Family Shepherd Conference Manual, 1993. Little Rock, AK.

Mentoring, Tape by Howard Hendricks, 1994. Workshop Dallas Theological Seminary, Dallas, TX.

*The Monitoring the Future Surveys*, Survey Research Center at the University of Michigan.

National Survey of Men, 1993-1998. Promise Keepers, Denver, CO.

Promise Keepers Surveys, March, June, 1999. Promise Keepers, Denver, CO.

U.S. Bureau of the Census, *Current Population Reports*, Series P20-514, *Marital Status and Living Arrangements:* March 1998.

U. S. Bureau of the Census, Unmarried-Couple Households, by Presence of Children: 1960 – Present, January 7, 1999.

CPSIA information can be obtained at www.ICGtesting.com
Printed in the USA
LVOW13s1122090614

389221LV00001B/78/A